Reflections

on Automotive History

VOLUME II

Bill Vance

Eramosa Valley Publishing

Canadian Cataloguing in Publication Data

Vance, Bill, 1935-
    Reflections on automotive history, volume II

Includes index.

ISBN   0-9698922-2-5 (case bound)
        0-9698922-3-3 (soft bound)

1. Automobiles — History. I. Title.

TL15.V35 1994   629.222'09
C94-932460-4 rev.

Printed in Canada by
Ampersand Printing
123 Woolwich Street
Guelph, Ontario N1H 3V1
Telephone (519) 836-8800
Fax (519) 836-7204

Additional copies can be obtained from
Eramosa Valley Publishing
Box 370
Rockwood, Ontario, Canada
N0B 2K0
Telephone: (519) 856-1065
Facisimile: (519) 856-2991

Cover: 1948 Cadillac

Photo Credits
All photos by the author, except the following pages:
    DaimlerChrysler AG 10, 14, 49 (both), 50, 52
    Ford Motor Company 18, 137
    General Motors Corporation cover, 26, 34, 103, 129
    General Motors of Canada 40, 46
    Grainger, David 175
    Honda Motor Company 78
    Mort, Norm 76
    Spiegelman, Richard 90 (right)
    Toronto Public Library 180
    Volkswagen AG 67 (right)

To Beth,
for her inspiration, encouragement
and unflagging support

TABLE OF CONTENTS

FOREWORD

Reflections on Automotive History, Volume II, is comprised of three sections: The Founders of the North American Automobile Industry's Big Three; An Overview of the European and Asian Automobile Industries; and A Diverse Collection of Cars and Companies.

In the Founders section readers would expect to find three men, the founders of General Motors, Ford and Chrysler, but I have expanded the section from three to five.

General Motors is the world's largest automobile manufacturer, with many outstanding leaders in its long and significant history. During its life three men have had a profound impact on the corporation. Although William Durant was GM's founder, two other men, Alfred P. Sloan, Jr., and Samuel McLaughlin, so strongly influenced its survival and growth in the United States, Canada, and other counties, that I have also included them.

Germany was the birthplace of the internal combustion engined automobile, and Japan brought it to new levels of production and refinement. This is explored in the overview of the evolution of the European and Asian automobile industries. From the engine pioneers and the first tentative steps at car-making by Karl Benz and Gottlieb Daimler, to the tiny Austin Seven and mighty Bugatti Royale, to the trend-setting, cross-engine, front-drive Mini, it's an eclectic journey.

The third section, which covers everything from the King Midget micro-car to Chrysler's futuristic turbine cars, is somewhat reminiscent of Volume I. Overall, readers will find Volume II different from Volume I, which contained 61 chapters that were expanded and revised versions of my newspaper columns. Volume I was published in response to reader requests, and was warmly received.

We would like to acknowledge the valuable assistance provided by several people. Richard Carroll, keen-eyed copy editor, stickler for good grammar, and knowledgable automobile person, made an invaluable contribution. To those corporations and individuals who provided photographs, I say thank you. And as always, to the ever helpful folks at Ampersand Printing in Guelph, Ontario, particularly Carolyn Klymko, goes our most heartfelt appreciation.

I hope you enjoy reading Volume II as much as I enjoyed writing it.

Bill Vance
Rockwood, Ontario
May, 2000

Founders of the
North American
Automobile Industry's Big Three

Walter P. Chrysler

WALTER PERCY CHRYSLER: 1875 – 1940
CHRYSLER CORPORATION

Three significant events in the history of the American automobile industry occurred in 1908: William Durant founded General Motors; Henry Ford introduced his Model T; and Walter Chrysler bought his first car.

Now, buying a car may not sound as though it ranks with starting a company, or introducing the second most popular car in history. But it nevertheless consolidated automobile interest in Walter Chrysler's mind, one that would ultimately result in the Chrysler Corporation, which became, along with General Motors and Ford, the third leg of America's Big Three automakers.

Walter Percy Chrysler was born in 1875 and grew up on a farm near Ellis, Kansas. His life was that of a typical farm boy, one of early mornings and hard work. He peddled milk, worked in a grocery store, played sports and enjoyed music.

Walter's father was an engineer with the Kansas Pacific Railroad, later part of the Union Pacific, and this no doubt helped instill in young Walter his avid interest in machinery. He read *Scientific American* magazine, hung around the railroad yard, and upon graduation from high school got a job in the railroad roundhouse. He started as a sweeper, but was soon able to begin his machinist's apprenticeship, becoming a journeyman in 1895.

To improve his knowledge and hone his skills Walter worked for several railway companies around the mid-west. By 1908 he was employed by the Union Pacific Railroad in Olwein, Iowa, and it was from here that he journeyed to the Chicago automobile show. He was already beginning to sense that railroading's future may be on the wane, that the automobile was the way of the future.

Walter was smitten by a big Locomobile car that was on display. He decided that he must have it, and although it was priced at $5000, he managed to arrange a loan for its purchase, and have the car shipped to Olwein. His wife, the former Della Forker whom he had married in 1901, didn't quite share Walter's enthusiasm. He detected that the kitchen door slammed a little harder than usual.

Walter had not bought the Locomobile to drive, but to take apart and study. He wanted to learn how it was made, the materials and machining that went into it. He disassembled it and re-assembled it in his barn, in the process becoming a kind of amateur automotive engineer. It was knowledge that would stand him in good stead in the future.

Life in the railroad went on, and Walter's skills, ambition and leadership qualities landed him the job of manager of the American Locomotive Company's manufacturing plant in Allegheny, Pennsylvania. It was here that his career would take its turn toward the automobile industry.

One of American Locomotive's board members was a man named James J. Storrow, a banker from Boston who also sat on the General Motors board of directors. He had assumed the position of interim president of General Motors for a short period after the banks took control from Billy Durant in 1910, and was still guiding its management. He had been impressed with the way Chrysler had managed American Locomotive's plant, turning it from a money loser into a profitable operation.

When the bankers took over GM, Buick was its most successful and profitable division. Its general manager was the conservative Charles Nash, who had started as an upholstery stuffer with the Durant-Dort Carriage Company, and worked his way up to vice-president. Billy Durant had hired him for General Motors.

James Storrow recommended Walter Chrysler to Nash as Buick's works manager. Nash was able to hire him at $6000 per year, half his railroad salary, indicating how badly Chrysler wanted to get into the automobile business. Nash was made president of GM in 1912, but retained his position as general manager of Buick.

By 1915 Durant was back in control of General Motors, and Nash didn't want to work for him again. He resigned from GM in 1916 and purchased the Thomas B. Jeffery Company of Kenosha, Wisconsin. Jeffery had made the Rambler car from 1902 to 1913, then changed the name to the Jeffery. Charles Nash changed Jeffery to the Nash Motor Company, and the cars became Nashes in 1917.

Nash wasn't the only one who didn't like working for Durant. Upon Nash's departure Walter Chrysler was made general manager of Buick, but he was becoming more and more dissatisfied with Durant's interference in Buick's management. Finally Chrysler resigned from GM in 1919. This time it was Walter Chrysler who was slamming the door. It was called the sound that was heard throughout the industry.

Chrysler said he was retired, but colleagues didn't believe it; at only 44 he still had a lot of energy left, and wasn't the kind of man to sit around and do nothing. Chrysler's reputation as an outstanding manager was well known, and he was soon approached by the bankers to take over the management of the failing Willys-Overland Company of Toledo, Ohio.

W-O had flourished on war contracts during the Great War, but when peace came, founder John North Willys had fallen into the same trap as Durant. He had made many acquisitions, and brought them together under the Willys Corporation. He became over-extended financially, and had not been as diligent in its management as he should have.

The whole enterprise was on the verge of bankruptcy. Chrysler had a good hand to play, and he played it well. He asked for a cool million dollars a year on a two year contract, and the right to build a car bearing his own name, should he decide to stay on indefinitely. He got both.

Through staff reduction, equipment sales, negotiations with suppliers, and sharp cost control, including cutting the salary of John Willys in half, Walter Chrysler was able to get W-O on the road to health. Before his second year was completed, he was invited to take on a new challenge, re-organizing the floundering Maxwell-Chalmers partnership, while continuing to work on W-O's recovery.

During his Willys-Overland period at its Elizabeth, New Jersey plant, Chrysler became acquainted with a bright three-man engineering team. Their names were Fred Zeder, Owen Skelton and Carl Breer, and working as a team they seemed to generate an engineering synergism that none could have achieved on his own. They were working on a new mid-priced car for W-O. Its design intrigued Chrysler, giving him a deep appreciation for the skills of the Zeder-Skelton-Breer unit.

W-O, however, could not afford to develop the Z-S-B design and bring it to production. In fact to raise capital it had to sell the Elizabeth plant. Walter Chrysler tried to buy it for the production of a Chrysler car, but was outbid by his old nemesis, Billy Durant. With the factory Durant also got the Z-S-B designed car, which he brought to market as the Flint. Zeder, Skelton and Breer left and incorporated themselves as a consulting engineering company.

Unable to acquire W-O's Elizabeth plant, Chrysler signed on to a two-year deal with the bankers to manage the troubled Maxwell Motor Corporation of Detroit. It had an association with the Chalmers Motor Car Company in which both companies manufactured cars in the same Highland Park, Michigan, plant. Maxwell would formally take over Chalmers in 1922, and the last Chalmers car appeared in 1923.

Walter Chrysler was becoming more savvy in business matters, and took the Maxwell job at a relatively low salary of $200,000 per year, but with generous stock options. Chrysler's first step was to get a fresh start by dissolving the Maxwell Motor Company and replacing it with the Maxwell Motor Corporation, with himself as chairman.

Walter P. Chrysler with first 1924 Chrysler car

One of Chrysler's immediate tasks was to get rid of a huge inventory of unsold Maxwells that he had inherited. Maxwells were noted for their fragile rear axles, and Chrysler had the axles of every one of the inventoried cars reinforced. To make the point he marketed them as "The Good Maxwell," and made a profit on them, albeit modest.

Chrysler then set out to develop new cars for the Maxwell Corporation, and had not forgotten the special talents of Zeder, Skelton and Breer. He was successful in luring them to Detroit to work for him. They became known as "The Three Musketeers," and their association with Chrysler would prove to be long and mutually beneficial.

What could have been a new Chalmers turned out to be the 1924 Chrysler, although it was a more advanced car. Zeder, Skelton and Breer fitted it with four-wheel hydraulic brakes, which had made their appearance on a production car, the Duesenberg, just two years earlier.

The Chrysler was powered by a side-valve, six cylinder engine which was a study in solid engineering. It had seven main bearings and full pressure lubrication. A vibration damper was fitted to the front of the crankshaft to reduce engine shake. The combustion chamber shape was based on principles laid down by Harry Ricardo, the pioneering English combustion engineer. This allowed a higher than normal compression ratio for greater specific power and better fuel economy. Its many advanced technical features began Chrysler's reputation for sound engineering.

But while Walter Chrysler now had a fine car bearing his own name, he wasn't about to stop. He wanted more than just a car with a Chrysler badge on it; he wanted his own company. By selling his General Motors stock, marshalling other assets, and obtaining some bank loans, Chrysler managed to gain control of the Maxwell Corporation. In June 1925 he changed it into the Chrysler Corporation, headquartered in Highland Park, Michigan. Within weeks Chrysler Canada was established in Windsor, Ontario. Walter Chrysler's dream was finally realized.

Walter Chrysler didn't reduce his pace once he got the Chrysler Corporation founded. He began expanding and diversifying his products just as Billy Durant had done with General Motors, although Chrysler was a much more attentive manager than Durant.

1928 Plymouth PA, moved Chrysler into the Big Three

The last year for the Maxwell name was 1925, but the car reappeared in 1926 as the four cylinder Chrysler 58 (the model number denoted top speed). There was also the original Chrysler, the 70, with a slightly larger engine, and there was a new, bigger, more luxurious Imperial 80 series. With the Imperial, Chrysler was moving into Packard and Peerless territory.

Dodge Brothers of Detroit had been manufacturing cars since 1914, and had built a reputation for sound if unexciting products. Horace and John Dodge had both died in 1920, and by the mid-1920s Dodge Brothers was in the hands of the bankers. Wanting to add a mid-range car to

his line, Walter Chrysler began negotiations to purchase Dodge, but a deal could not be consummated.

Unable to buy Dodge, Chrysler went ahead with the development of his own mid-market car, the DeSoto. This set the stage for another momentous period in the life of the Chrysler Corporation.

Nineteen-twenty-eight was the young Chrysler Corporation's pivotal year. The Dodge bankers had a change of heart and Dodge Brothers became available to Chrysler, who purchased it. This left Chrysler with two mid-range cars, the Dodge and DeSoto, so Chrysler dropped the lowest priced Dodge to make a place for DeSoto. In 1933 they would reverse places in the company's hierarchy, with DeSoto moving above Dodge in price.

The acquisition of Dodge gave Chrysler two important assets: Dodge's extensive production facilities, and its well established dealer network. It also added trucks to the Chrysler Corporation's offerings because Dodge had taken over the Graham brothers' truck building operation in 1926.

1937 Chrysler Airflow

In addition to acquiring Dodge and launching the DeSoto, Chrysler had one more announcement in 1928. This was the introduction of the new, low priced Plymouth. New may be somewhat of a misnomer, because the Plymouth was really the re-badged Chrysler 50 four cylinder, which itself could trace its lineage back to Maxwell.

The new Plymouth was well engineered and priced competitively. It provided Chrysler with a car capable of giving strong competition to the Ford Motor Company and General Motors, rising to third in industry sales behind the Ford and Chevrolet in 1932. It was instrumental in making Chrysler one of the American Big Three car companies.

As a little icing on the cake, in 1928 two Chryslers finished a surprising 3rd and 4th in the famous LeMans, France, 24-hour endurance race. It would be the best American car showing until 1953 when American millionaire sportsman Briggs Cunningham's Cunningham finished 3rd. Interestingly, it was powered by a Chrysler engine.

The Chrysler Corporation managed to cope with its newfound expansion. Then in 1929 the business scene changed with the stock market crash which ushered in the Depression, which hit all automakers. Thanks to a broad product line, a good engineering reputation, and Walter Chrysler's well proved ability to run a tight ship, Chrysler would survive the Depression.

Chrysler would step out ahead in styling in 1934 with the radical Airflow, available as both a Chrysler and DeSoto models. In spite of such advanced engineering features as between-the-axles seating, made possible by the forward engine placement, and sturdy semi-unit body construction with an internal "cage," the Airflow failed in the marketplace. Customers were not ready to accept the swoopy, art deco styling. The Airflow would be offered only until 1937.

In 1935 Walter Chrysler handed the reins of Chrysler's presidency to assistant K.T. Kellar so that he could concentrate on the chairmanship. He would cease active participation in company affairs in 1938 for health reasons, and died in 1940 at the age of only 65. With his passing the American automobile industry lost one of its true pioneers.

Henry Ford I

Henry Ford: 1863 – 1947
Ford Motor Company

When the definitive history of the twentieth century is written, Henry Ford's name will figure prominently. His impact and contribution have been among the greatest in what has been called the century of oil. It was he, more than any other man, who put North America and much of the rest of the world on wheels.

While the automobile was European by invention, it was the United States and Canada that popularized it, transforming it from a plaything of the rich to a utilitarian implement of business and pleasure. In the vast reaches of North America it became a necessity.

The vehicle that contributed the most to making this possible was Henry Ford's Model T. It was not only durable, simple and cheap to buy, but for most of the 19 years it was produced, it was made on the moving automobile assembly line which Ford pioneered. And the huge Ford River Rouge car manufacturing plant became a model for other giant production enterprises.

It all started when Henry was born on a farm in Dearborn, Michigan, just west of Detroit, in 1863. His father William's family had emigrated from Ireland in 1847, fleeing the great Irish potato famine. William's brothers had come in the 1830s, so there was already an established Ford clan when he arrived.

The Fords were enterprising and hard working. When they arrived in America they eschewed the dirty, grinding factory life of the industrial cities like New York and Boston, and headed for what was then the Michigan frontier where life was rugged but independence was valued. Land was cheap and they cleared the forests, built homes, established farms and raised families.

William Ford worked as a carpenter and saved enough money to buy his own land. In 1861 he married Margaret Litogot O'Hearn, the daughter of his employer, and they settled into farming life. Their son Henry, the first of six children, was born on July 30, 1863.

Although the Ford's were, by the standards of the time, prosperous farmers, as young Henry grew up he wanted to leave what he saw as the boredom of agricultural life. He had a strong interest in, and aptitude for, mechanical things, and it was apparent from an early age that some day Henry would leave the farm. It was no surprise, therefore, that when he was just 16, he walked the nine miles to Detroit and began serving his apprenticeship as a machinist with the Flower Brothers' machine shop.

It was a good shop in which to train. It was well equipped and made a variety of iron and brass products such as valves, fire hydrants and steam whistles. Another notable auto pioneer who learned his craft there was David Dunbar Buick who would go on to found a successful plumbing business, before going into automobiles.

Henry then moved to the Detroit Dry Dock Co. where he completed his apprenticeship in 1882, before the age of 20. He then did a surprising thing; he succumbed to his father's urging and moved back to the farm where he stayed until he was almost 30. During that period he operated a threshing machine powered by a Westinghouse steam engine. Henry became so proficient that he was soon a Westinghouse service representative.

By 1891 the call of the city was again too strong to resist, and Henry and his wife, the former Clara Bryant, whom he had married in 1888, moved back to Detroit where he took a job as a mechanic with the Edison Illuminating Co. He was soon promoted to chief engineer, and it was while working with Edison that he began building the gasoline engine that he would use to power his car.

In a small red brick building at the rear of 58 Bagley Avenue in Detroit where he and Clara lived, Henry Ford and his assistant Charles King constructed his first car. King was also working on his own "car," a wagon with a engine attached to it, and on March 6, 1896, would become the first man to drive a self propelled gasoline engined vehicle in Detroit.

Henry Ford called his car a quadricycle, an apt name because it resembled two bicycles held together by a frame. The small two cylinder gasoline engine that Henry built was mounted at the rear and drove the wheels via a chain. A two-passenger seat was fitted in the middle, steering was by a tiller, and there was even a "horn," a household doorbell mounted on the dashboard at the front.

As the little 500-pound (227 kg) vehicle neared completion and the time approached to test it, Henry became more and more obsessed. In early June 1896 he worked almost continuously for two days. Finally early in the morning of June 4th it was ready for a test drive. There was one last surprise. It was the classic tale of the boat in the basement; the quadricycle would not go through the door of the little "factory." Undeterred, Henry picked up an axe and knocked out the doorjamb and enough bricks to allow the machine to pass through.

The test drive was reasonably successful, but because of the lack of any advance publicity the

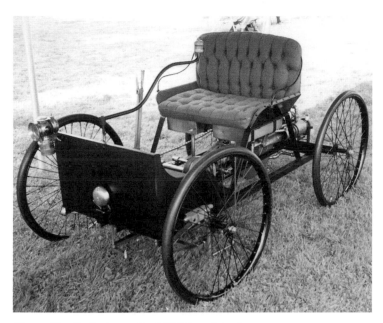

Henry Ford's first car, the 1896 Quadricycle

racing car. When completed in the fall of 1901 he raced it against Alexander Winton of Cleveland. He beat the favoured Winton and gained national recognition.

Henry Ford's racing success attracted sufficient financial backing from Detroit businessmen to form another company in November, 1901, called the Henry Ford Company, with Henry as chief engineer. Alas Henry was too interested in racing, and soon split with his new partners. They turned to machinery wizard and master of precision Henry Leland to run the firm, and renamed it the Cadillac Automobile Co.

Ford returned to building another race car, the result being the huge "999" single seater in which a courageous bicycle racer named Barney Oldfield beat all comers in an August, 1902 race. He averaged almost 60 mph (96 km/h) in the process.

This fame brought yet another backer in the form of Detroit coal dealer Alexander Malcomson and together they formed the Ford Motor Co. in June 1903. Henry was now ready to settle into passenger cars, and his third attempt was successful. The following year, on August 17, 1904, The Ford Motor Co. of Canada was established in Walkerville, now part of Windsor, Ontario, by Gordon McGregor of the Walkerville Wagon Works.

Ford Motor Co.'s first plant was set up on Mack Avenue in Detroit. An order for 650

event went unreported. Ford continued to improve the quadricycle, eventually sold it, and began work on a second car which was completed in 1898.

This resulted in newspaper coverage which attracted the attention of a wealthy businessman named William Murphy. Murphy financed the establishment in 1900 of Detroit's first car manufacturer, the Detroit Automobile Company, with Henry Ford as its superintendent. Unfortunately its products were expensive and laborious to build, and did not sell well. The company lasted only nine months.

Ford then turned his attention to building a

1903 Ford Model A, Ford's first production car

engines and drivelines was placed with the machine shop of Horace and John Dodge, who would later form their own car company. Bodies and tires were also ordered locally, and the enterprise began assembly of the Ford Model A.

Three critically important staff acquisitions were made early in the company's history: Charles Sorensen, James Couzens and Childe Harold Wills. Wills was an accomplished engineer, and Couzens was a shrewd businessman who had moved to Detroit from Canada. His sharp accounting and business discipline were invaluable in the success of the Ford Motor Co.

Harold Wills's gifted engineering skill gave

Henry Ford's intuitive mechanical ideas substance. He was instrumental in introducing strong and durable vanadium steel to Ford's cars.

Charles Sorensen, a Danish-born pattern-maker who joined Ford in 1905, was also able to convert Henry's intuition and simple descriptions into reality. His outstanding ability to make wooden casting patterns for cast iron parts earned him the nickname "Cast Iron Charlie." He would become Ford's right-hand man and chief executive officer, and serve the company for almost 40 years.

To gain further publicity for the company, Henry Ford once again built a racing car, the Arrow, a twin of the huge and crude 999. When Barney Oldfield wasn't available to drive it on a record run, Henry drove it himself over the ice of Lake St. Clair. Although he almost frightened himself to death in the process, on January 12, 1904, Henry covered a mile in 39.4 seconds, a speed of 91.37 mph (147 km/h). He thereby became the holder of the world's land speed record. Although the record was broken only 10 days later by William K. Vanderbilt in a Mercedes, it added to the Ford mystique, and boosted his company's profile.

Business flourished, and they moved into larger premises on Piquette Avenue in Detroit in 1905. But while the company was thriving, all was not settled in Henry Ford's mind. Although his desire was to build a light inexpensive car for the common man, his financial backers were pushing him into heavier, more luxurious cars. The 1906 six cylinder Model K Ford, for example, was an expensive ($2500) car. It was out of step with Ford's belief at that time that "A car should not have any more cylinders than a cow has teats."

Ford was finally able to shake free after an angry encounter, following which Malcomson sold his Ford stock in 1906. Henry could now pursue the kind of car he wanted. Models N, R and S of 1906-07 were much closer to Henry's philosophy.

In the winter of 1906-07 Henry had Sorensen partition off a room on the top floor of the Piquette Avenue plant. There, Henry, Sorensen and a few trusted assistants designed the Model T Ford. It looked tall and spindly, but its vanadium steel made it deceptively strong. It was powered by a 20-horsepower four cylinder engine, had a foot-shifted planetary transmission that was easy to operate, and was exactly the kind of car that North America needed.

The Model T was introduced late in 1908 as a 1909 model. It was all that Henry hoped it would be. It could attain about 45 mph (72 km/h), give 20 to 25 mpg, and had enough ground clearance to be useful on poor rural roads.

Sales of Model Ts were so brisk that the company couldn't turn them out fast enough. A new larger plant was constructed in Highland Park, and during 1910, its first year of production, it turned out 19,000 Model Ts, followed by almost 35,000 the following year.

Henry was already becoming established as an American folk hero, but his resistance to the Selden patent consolidated it. In 1895 a Rochester, New York, patent lawyer by the name of George Selden was granted a patent for a horseless carriage driven by an internal combustion engine. Selden did not construct such a vehicle. Through some dealings the patent ended up in the hands of an organization calling itself the Association of Licensed Automobile Manufacturers.

Other manufacturers buckled under, joining the ALAM and paying a royalty on each car. Ford resisted, and finally defeated the Selden patent in a 1911 court ruling. Ford was ecstatic, and the future looked boundless.

Ford's problem with the Model T was that they couldn't make enough of them. In 1908 Charles Sorensen and some assistants had experimented with a crude type of moving assembly line by pulling a chassis past piles of parts, and attaching them as it moved past. The explosive success of the Model T, however, had shelved the assembly line until they were in the new Highland Park plant.

Once Model T production was humming along in the new plant, Sorensen again began experimenting with the moving line, with Henry

1914 Ford Model T, a car for the masses

Ford's blessing. After much planning and many trials and shifting of manpower, the moving assembly line was installed at Ford in 1913. Output escalated from 170,000 Model Ts in 1912, to over half a million in 1915.

Ford again outgrew its premises so Henry had the vast new River Rouge factory constructed. It was the biggest manufacturing plant in the world, and the company was so powerful, so vertically integrated, that iron, coal and timber from Ford's own mines and forests came in one end of the Rouge, and Model Ts drove out the other.

As Model T production increased, Henry Ford reduced the price, reaching a low of $295. Ford was convinced that those who built his cars should also be able to afford them, so in 1914 he raised the daily pay rate of his employees to five dollars. Business rivals predicted chaos, but the result was the opposite.

While Henry Ford was a mechanical genius, and a folk hero, he had his dark side. He was quite ignorant in matters outside his narrow area of expertise. He was often mean and vindictive, and enjoyed pitting his executives against one another. The strong willed and sometimes pugnacious Sorensen was the one man that he couldn't intimidate, and as Henry grew older Sorensen was in effect running the company.

Henry named his only child, son Edsel, president of the Ford Motor Co. in 1919, but it was a sham. Henry continued to call the shots, undermining and countermanding Edsel whenever he could. There are many who believe that it led to Edsel's early death in 1943 at age 50.

When Model T sales began to flag in the mid-twenties, Ford reluctantly agreed to replace it. The Model A was the result, and was built from 1928 to 1932.

When Chevrolet introduced its new six cylinder car in 1929 it caught Ford with its four cylinder Model A. Many buyers preferred the smoothness and power of six cylinders, so Henry decided to go Chevrolet one better and move to an eight.

The new Ford V-8 arrived in 1932, and although

there were some teething problems, it was a sensation. Sorensen had done a masterful job of producing a V-8 engine block that could be cast in one piece. It was compact, smooth and powerful, and brought eight cylinder power to the popular priced field. It was Henry Ford's last technological triumph.

As Henry grew older he became senile and cantankerous. With the death of Edsel in 1943 Henry assumed full control of the company, although it was evident that he wasn't capable of running an enterprise as vast and complex as the Ford Motor Co. He had alienated Sorensen and forced him to leave.

Henry was coming more and more under the influence of Harry Bennett, much to the chagrin of Sorensen before he left, and the Ford family. Bennett ran Ford's internal security force known as the Service Department. He was a man of questionable morality and a very shady past, and he aspired to the presidency of Ford.

The Ford Motor Co. was deeply involved in war work, and both the Ford family and the government were concerned about its chaotic management, and its ultimate viability. The result was that Henry's grandson Henry Ford II, Edsel's son, was released from the navy and made president of Ford. Old Henry protested, but the Ford women, his wife Clara and Edsel's widow Eleanor, "convinced" him of the wisdom of stepping aside.

1932 Ford V-8 convertible coupe, eight cylinder power at a popular price

Henry Ford II was only 26, but he was wise enough to hire the most competent managers he could find, some from other companies, and some who were leaving the armed services. Under Henry Ford II the Ford Motor Co. was put back on its feet.

Henry Ford the first died in 1947 at the age of 84. His life had reached almost mythical proportions, but he left this earth in his Fair Lane home by the dim light of candles, the way he had entered it. In a final twist of irony for a man who excelled at things mechanical, his beloved electrical generating plant had been flooded out by the rising Rouge River.

William C. Durant

William Crapo Durant: 1861 – 1947
General Motors Corporation

William (Billy) Durant was a visionary, a man who saw opportunity where others didn't. He had the drive and initiative to capitalize on his hunches, and the personal charisma to sweep those around him into his orbit. These qualities would lead him to found what would become the world's mightiest enterprise: the General Motors Corporation.

Billy came with some good bloodlines. His mother Rebecca was the daughter of Henry Howland Crapo, who had moved from New Bedford, Massachusetts, to the small Michigan city of Flint in 1856. In addition to being successful in several businesses in New Bedford, Crapo had been its town clerk, treasurer and tax collector. He was already in his fifties when he moved to Flint, and although his children were grown, most followed him.

In Michigan Crapo continued to demonstrate his popular leadership qualities. He successfully established himself in the booming Michigan lumber business, and was soon elected mayor of Flint, then a senator, and ultimately the governor of Michigan. He died in 1869, but his outstanding reputation lived on in Flint.

One who hadn't relocated to Flint with the family was Rebecca, now Mrs. William Clark Durant. Durant was a clerk with the National Webster Bank of Boston. They had a daughter Rebecca, and a son, William Crapo Durant, born in the Durant home in Boston on December 8, 1861.

When Rebecca's marriage to William Durant failed she took her two children Rebecca and little Billy to Flint and settled there in 1872. Billy was seven, and although his father was no longer present, the Crapo family had many prominent members in Flint who provided a nurturing environment for the boy.

Billy grew up with the normal activities of youth. He played sports, dabbled in music, and then, much to his mother's chagrin, dropped out of high school at 18, just six months short of graduation.

After a stint at the Crapo Lumber Co., which had been established by his grandfather, Billy moved on to become a successful cigar salesman, and then secretary of Flint's private waterworks. He reorganized the waterworks into an efficient operation, and became well known around town.

He moved from this to selling insurance, and with a partner had soon developed one of the biggest brokerages in central Michigan. Then he had his encounter with young Johnny Alger's road cart.

Alger, who worked in the hardware store of Billy's friend Dallas Dort, offered Billy a ride in his new two-wheeled, horse-drawn road cart, not much more than a racing sulky. Billy accepted, and was mightily impressed with the comfort of the ride provided by the novel seat suspension.

Durant was so excited about the little road cart that he wanted to meet its manufacturer and explore getting into the business. He boarded the train that night for Coldwater, Michigan, some 120 miles (193 km) southwest of Flint. The next morning he was at the office of the Coldwater Road Car Co., builder of the little two-wheeler.

Durant talked to the owners. Would they sell him a small interest in the business? Somewhat disillusioned with the operation, partners Thomas O'Brien and William Schmedlen offered to sell Durant the whole operation, including plans, materials and unfinished carts. Negotiations resulted in the consummation of a deal in which Durant would buy the business, including the seat suspension patent, for $1,500.

Billy didn't have anything like $1,500, but he was able to arrange a bank loan for $2,000, enough to pay for the company and move it to Flint. His friend Dallas Dort, wanting out of the hardware business, came in as a partner, and the Flint Road Cart Co. was born in September 1886.

Durant was soon on the road enthusiastically marketing their new product. He displayed it at the state fair in Madison, Wisconsin, where it won a blue ribbon. Billy then visited several implement dealers, and by the time he returned home he had orders for 600 road carts.

But the Flint Road Car Co. hadn't built one cart yet! It was typical of the way Billy operated, and undismayed, he contracted with William Paterson of Flint to build 1200 carts. Paterson, a transplanted Canadian, had learned the carriage business in Guelph, Ontario, and had moved to Michigan where he developed into Flint's largest buggy maker. He agreed to build Durant and Dort the road carts for $12.50 each; they were able to sell them for about twice that.

The Flint Road Cart Co. was formally incorporated in 1893, and the name was changed to the Durant-Dort Carriage Co. in 1895. Through aggressive salesmanship, and vertical integration, which included the production of its own axles, wheels, buggy tops, and paints and varnishes, and even owning its own forests, Durant-Dort grew into the largest carriage company in the U.S.

Billy was a millionaire by his early forties. But he was getting restless; he was a creator, not a manager, and the carriage business was humming along very successfully.

Then came his encounter with Dr. Herbert

Hills. In an event reminiscent of his ride in Johnny Alger's road cart 18 years earlier, in September, 1904 Billy went for a ride in Dr. Hills's new Buick, the first production Buick built in Flint. Durant then took it out for an afternoon by himself; by the time he returned he had changed his mind about the automobile. He no longer saw it as a smelly, noisy contraption, but now recognized its potential for personal transportation. Billy was sold on the car.

The Buick Motor Co. had been incorporated in Detroit in 1903 to manufacture engines. It was backed by two brothers, Ben and Frank Briscoe, makers of sheetmetal products. David Buick, a successful plumbing equipment producer who had invented a method of affixing porcelain to cast iron, was also a partner. Buick fell into debt to the Briscoes from which he couldn't extricate himself, and lost control of the company to them.

The Buick Motor Co. didn't prosper, and desperate to rid themselves of the money-loser, the Briscoes offered to sell it to the Flint Wagon Works. James Whiting, a director of Flint Wagon Works was anxious to get into the automobile business, and promoted the purchase. The result was that the Flint Wagon Works bought Buick and moved it to Flint late in 1903. Ben Briscoe would go on to join with Jonathan Maxwell to form the Maxwell-Briscoe car company; the Maxwell was the forerunner of Chrysler.

Buick produced its first Flint-built automobile in 1904. It was powered by a valve-in-head engine developed by Buick engineers, Walter Marr and Eugene Richard. It was more efficient and powerful than the then common side-valve engine, and it would become a famous Buick trademark.

But in spite of its good engine, the Buick Motor Co. was soon in deeper debt than the Flint Wagon Works could sustain. It was decided that if there was one person who could save Buick, it was Billy Durant. Billy had been spending a lot of time in New York investing, some would say speculating, in the stock market. He was invited back to Flint by his old friends who were trying to rescue Buick. This led to Billy's ride in Dr. Hills's Buick, and his conversion on that September day in 1904.

Dallas Dort agreed with Billy on the future of the car, and with Durant-Dort's backing Durant took over the Buick Motor Co. and re-capitalised it. Although Buick hadn't built more than 40 cars, the reinvigorated Billy displayed a Buick at the New York auto show where he received more than 1000 orders. It was the road cart story all over again – sell them and then figure out how to build them. Billy loved it.

With Billy's drive and charisma, Buick's strong overhead valve engine, and the Durant-Dort dealer network, Buick was soon thriving. To demonstrate its speed, Billy organized the Buick racing team starring such outstanding drivers as

1905 Buick, Durant's building block for General Motors

T. Whereas Ford saw the future in one sound, inexpensive design replicated in the millions, Durant foresaw a market for a variety of cars from low priced to luxury.

Billy began to build his dream. After an unsuccessful attempt to consolidate Buick, Olds, Ford and Maxwell-Briscoe into one company, Durant incorporated a holding company in New Jersey called General Motors Co. (later corporation) on September 16, 1908.

Billy brought Buick into GM on October 1st, and using it as his anchor, began assembling companies under the

Louis Chevrolet and "Wild Bob" Burman, and it enjoyed wide success.

By 1907 Buick's annual production exceeded 4600, second in the industry only to Henry Ford's almost 15,000. Flint looked like a mining town as Buick workers streamed into town and lived in tents, shacks and even packing cases until housing could be built.

But Billy the builder wasn't about to relax. His vision of the car was much broader than that of Henry Ford, who was about to launch his Model

GM umbrella. He soon purchased Olds, and tried to buy the Albert Champion Co., makers of spark plugs. When this failed he hired Albert Champion himself and brought him to Flint where he set up the Champion Ignition Co., later the AC Spark Plug division of General Motors.

The Oakland Motor Car Co. (later Pontiac) of Pontiac, Michigan was the next purchase. Cadillac, which had a reputation for high quality engineering, was soon added. Within two years Durant had bought or taken a financial position in some two dozen car, truck and component companies for General Motors. These included the McLaughlin Motor Car Co. of Oshawa, Ontario. Some, such as the Heany Lamp companies, would turn out to be expensive failures, but many, such as Buick, Olds, Cadillac and McLaughlin, were worthwhile, and formed the basis of the GM of today.

Alas, by 1910 GM was over-extended financially; it had grown so fast, and with so little central management, that Durant lost control to the bankers. Billy was made a vice-president of General Motors, but he was no longer in a position of power in the company he had created.

In the face of such a humiliating defeat, most men would have licked their wounds and quietly taken their pay. But not Billy. He still had his strong reputation in Flint, and within weeks had teamed up with ex-racer Louis Chevrolet and several Flint businessmen to form, among others, the Chevrolet Motor Co.

Louis Chevrolet designed a new car for Durant. Although it was bigger and more luxurious than he wanted, Durant had Chevrolet Motor Co. produce it. He was also instrumental in forming the Little Motor Car Co. to produce lighter cars, and the Mason Motor Co. to supply engines. Because Billy favoured lighter cars than the large one that Louis Chevrolet had designed, Chevrolet left the company and turned his hand to designing some very successful racing cars.

Billy was on a roll again. His Chevrolet Royal Mail roadster and Baby Grand touring cars were introduced late in 1913. With their jaunty styling and overhead valve engines they became quite popular. They replaced the Little cars, and with them, and the Four-Ninety model that came in 1915, Chevrolet prospered sufficiently that it enabled Durant to quietly amass General Motors stock.

Durant had never resigned his GM vice-presidency, although he had been inactive, and by September 16, 1915, exactly seven years after he had incorporated it, Billy regained control of his "baby," General Motors. He was assisted by Pierre S. duPont of the famous duPont chemical company, and others, but Durant was clearly the leader. The little Chevrolet company had swallowed giant General Motors.

In charge again, Billy took off on another round of activity. He changed the General Motors Company, registered in New Jersey, to the General Motors Corporation, registered in Delaware. He raised capitalization from $60 million to $100 million. He also set out on another spending binge. Among his projects was the forming of United Motors Company to control several component manufacturers, among them the Hyatt Roller Bearing Co., which Billy had acquired from owner Alfred P. Sloan, Jr.

Sloan, an engineer, had taken control of Hyatt in 1898, and through good management and the production of meticulously engineered products, had turned it into a thriving enterprise. Sloan was

1931 Durant phaeton, one of the last as Durant's dream ends

appointed president of United Motors, and would become the president of General Motors in the post-Durant era, brilliantly evolving it into a thriving, industry-dominating business.

Unfortunately, during his second tenure Billy's management style would result in the loss of some of GM's best managers. Charles Nash, GM president, resigned in 1916 and purchased the Thomas B.Jeffery Co., and re-named it the Nash Motor Co. Walter Chrysler, general manager of Buick, left in 1919, and would ultimately form the Chrysler Corp.

With Durant's change of GM from a holding company to a corporation, the subsidiaries became operating divisions. As the bankers gradually left the organization the division managers became the board of directors. Among the divisions was McLaughlin's Canadian operation, which Durant completed purchasing in 1918, and turned into General Motors of Canada.

As General Motors grew it became too complicated even for Durant's outstanding talent. His heavy involvement in the stock market also absorbed much of his attention. The result was that when the post-World War I downturn came in 1920, GM was in serious trouble. Production continued and inventories built up in the face of falling sales.

Led by the duPont interests, who were anxious to protect their investment in GM, Durant was ousted for the second and last time in 1920. It was a sad day, but he didn't brood over it. Within weeks he was back in the automobile business with his new company, Durant Motors, Inc.

Durant Motors would last until 1932, when it failed like so many others in the Depression. When Billy Durant died with little means in 1947 he was managing a Flint bowling alley, which, naturally, he was planning to turn into a national franchise. His legacy lives on as one of the great automobile titans of the twentieth century.

Alfred P. Sloan, Jr.

Alfred P. Sloan, Jr.: 1875 – 1966 General Motors Corporation

Strictly speaking, Alfred P. Sloan, Jr., wasn't the founder of General Motors. That honour goes to William "Billy" Crapo Durant, a personable and flamboyant carriage entrepreneur from Flint, Michigan, who registered GM as a holding company in the State of New Jersey on September 16, 1908.

But while Durant founded GM, and brought in some of the companies that would contribute to its later success, it is safe to say that if there hadn't been an Alfred P. Sloan, Jr., there wouldn't be a General Motors today. He was really its saviour in the early 1920s. He made such a significant contribution to the organization and development of General Motors that he deserves to be remembered as a kind of "second founder."

After setting up General Motors Durant quickly began building his empire, folding in Buick, which he already controlled, and adding such companies as Oldsmobile, Oakland (later Pontiac) and Cadillac to the enterprise. By 1910 he had over-extended GM, and was forced out of control of the company by the bankers, who took over its management. He stayed on as a vice-president, but with little power.

He then started the Chevrolet Motor Co., with one of his ex- Buick race drivers, Louis Chevrolet, and was able to make it so successful that he used its stock to regain control of GM in 1915. Billy returned to his old ways, going on another buying spree for GM, and among his purchases was the Hyatt Roller Bearing Company. What Durant got with it would prove to be something far more important than roller bearings: Hyatt's owner, Alfred P. Sloan, Jr.

Sloan was born in New Haven, Conn., on May 23, 1875, and graduated from the Massachusetts Institute of Technology with a degree in electrical engineering in 1895. His graduation coincided almost exactly with the emergence of the motor car in the United States, and he was destined to play a very significant role in its future development.

Following graduation Sloan went to work for Hyatt of Newark, N.J., as "a kind of office boy, draughtsman, salesman and general assistant to the enterprise," as he recounted in his 1963 autobiography, *My Years With General Motors*.

Not seeing much of a future for Hyatt, Sloan soon left to join an electric-refrigerator company that was trying "to supply centrally located electric refrigeration in apartment houses." He would stay there two years.

In the meantime, Hyatt's declining fortunes were vindicating Sloan's early assessment; by 1898 it had slipped to the verge of bankruptcy. At this point Sloan's father, a wholesaler of tea, coffee and cigars, and an associate, combined to invest $5,000 to rescue Hyatt. They made the investment on the condition that young Alfred would take it over on a six-month trial basis.

By the end of the period Hyatt showed a $12,000 profit under Sloan's stewardship, with prospects for continued expansion. As Sloan said in his book, "I could not know then that through Hyatt I had entered one of the headwaters of General Motors."

The growth of Hyatt and the motor industry paralleled each other. Under Sloan's general managership Hyatt's annual profit was up to $60,000 within five years. Sloan functioned not only as a salesman, but also a kind of consulting engineer to the auto industry regarding the use of Hyatt bearings. In his quest to sell bearings to the automobile manufacturers, Sloan got to know many of the early giants of the business such as Walter Chrysler, Billy Durant, Henry Ford, Sam McLaughlin, Charles Nash and Harold Wills.

In 1916, with Hyatt now flourishing through substantial business with the motor industry, Sloan got a surprising phone call from Durant of General Motors. Durant wanted to know if Sloan would consider selling Hyatt to GM. The idea came as a shock to Sloan, but when he considered the larger possibilities, and Hyatt's vulnerability in having only a few large customers, he accepted. In 1916 the Hyatt Roller Bearing Company became part of United Motors, a GM subsidiary which Durant had organized to buy a number of component companies. Already recognized for his management talent, Sloan was made president of United Motors.

Besides Hyatt, GM, through United Motors, bought the New Departure Manufacturing Co. a maker of ball bearings; the Remy Electric Co., maker of automobile ignition equipment; Perlman Rim Corp.; and Dayton Engineering Laboratories Co., known as Delco, another auto electric company.

With Delco, Durant made another outstanding acquisition in the person of Charles Kettering, Delco's owner. Kettering was the brilliant electrical engineer who had invented the electric self starter which was introduced on the 1912 Cadillac. He became GM's director of research, and in addition to the starter, he made many other important pioneering contributions to the automobile industry over the years in such areas as anti-knock gasoline, high compression engines, and two-stroke diesels.

It didn't take Sloan long to realize that Billy Durant's time out of control of GM hadn't changed him. He was the same charismatic, empire-building entrepreneur he had always been, and he had the same cavalier disregard for administrative matters. Since Sloan had a flair for orderly business, he was soon Durant's trusted aide and confidant. Given Durant's laissez-faire attitude, and his stock market activity, Sloan was virtually running the company, although without the authority.

The lack of organization in GM was anathema to Sloan's logical mind. Seeing his talent for business, Durant made Sloan head of a committee charged with preparing some operating guidelines for GM.

Sloan's "Organization Study," completed in late 1919, covered such matters as return on investment, profit centres, central control, and the allocation of resources based on the most efficiently operated divisions. It created a good balance between the extremes of centralization and decentralization.

Sloan presented his Organization Study to Durant in 1919, and again in 1920. Although Durant seemed to accept its recommendations, he did nothing to implement them. This was probably because, as an active stock market player, he had very pressing matters to deal with regarding his investment portfolio.

Durant would not be with GM to see the results of Sloan's work. A disastrous frenzy of overproduction in 1920 due to the lack of central control, and an economic downturn following World War I, almost brought GM down. Durant was forced out for the second and last time. The company again fell into the hands of the bankers, a replay of 1910, and Durant went on to form the Durant Motor Co., which would last until 1932.

The duPont Chemical Co. was a heavy investor in General Motors, and to protect its asset, Pierre duPont was named chairman and Sloan was appointed vice-president. In 1923 Sloan was elevated to the position of president of General Motors.

The duPont entry into active participation in GM management was the beginning of Sloan's golden era in which he would guide GM on its climb to supremacy. He correctly identified that the automobile business was changing from a "mass market," as exemplified by the Model T Ford, to what he called a "mass-class" market demanding more diversity and luxury. Sloan sensed that the days of Henry Ford's somewhat stark Model T would soon come to an end. His aim was to position GM to take advantage of the expanding and diverging market with an array of more comfortable, stylish cars. The Chevrolet was being aimed directly at Ford.

Alfred Sloan had his work cut out for him. In 1920, GM's share of the automobile market stood at 17 percent. With the recession and GM's poor

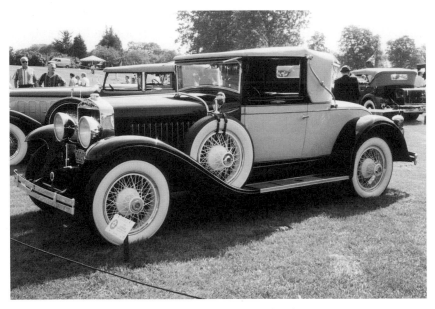

1927 LaSalle. Under Sloan, GM's LaSalle formalized automotive styling

were mechanically weak, had small dealer bodies, and were posting poor sales. There were also serious price overlaps throughout the line. And worst of all, of the 10 nameplates, only Buick and Cadillac were making a profit.

Sloan analyzed the line-up, and reduced the 10 marques down to five, in the process discontinuing the Scripps-Booth, Sheridan, two Oldsmobiles and one Chevrolet model. He organized the company's line of cars into five progressive, non-overlapping makes: Chevrolet; Oakland (later Pontiac); Oldsmobile, Buick, and Cadillac. They ranked from the popular priced Chevrolet, with its price lowered to better compete with Ford, to the luxurious Cadillac. Sloan now had the rational line of cars he wanted.

The annual model change that evolved under Sloan's reign was designed to encourage buyers to trade their cars in for new ones every few years. The hierarchy of marques encouraged buyers to move up the luxury ladder as their careers progressed, aspiring ultimately to a Cadillac. All of this was being facilitated by the increasing use of instalment buying. The General Motors Acceptance Corp., for example, had been established in 1919. And for those who couldn't afford new cars, there was the burgeoning used car market.

management it slipped to about 12 percent in 1921. Ford, meanwhile, with is vast River Rouge complex, and no serious competition for its Model T in the low priced class, went from 45 percent of the market in 1920, to 60 percent in 1921.

To counter this, and accommodate the new mass-class trend, Sloan's management set out to rationalize GM's car lineup. In 1921 GM had the following models: Chevrolet 490; Chevrolet FB; Oakland; Oldsmobiles with four, six and eight cylinders; Scripps-Booth; Sheridan; Buick; and Cadillac. In these 10 makes there were some, such as the Sheridan and the Scripps-Booth, that

To give substance to his evolving concept of the annual model change, Sloan reinforced the importance of styling diversity by establishing the Art and Colour Section under the direction of Harley Earl. Earl had come to GM's attention while working as a stylist to the stars in Hollywood, California, where he was creating custom cars for Don Lee, a Cadillac distributor.

Impressed with the stories that his senior staff brought back from California, Sloan engaged Earl on a contract to style Cadillac's new lower priced "companion" car to celebrate Cadillac's 25th anniversary. This was the 1927 LaSalle, and it proved so successful with its imaginative lines and dramatic use of colour that Sloan hired Earl permanently to set up the Art and Colour Section. It reported directly to Sloan, and provided styling services to all GM divisions. It was renamed the Styling Department in 1937.

Under Sloan, GM pulled out of its slump, and prospered greatly, continuing to earn a profit right through the Depression when most other car companies were losing money, or failing. He gradually brought some 50 percent of the North American automotive market under GM's control.

Sloan's organization study formed the basis for the operation of the corporation. It evolved autonomous divisions responsible for building vehicles and components, guided by a central coordinating authority that dealt with matters of corporate interest. It would become a model for large, diversified corporations.

General Motors also expanded internationally under Sloan, acquiring Vauxhall of England in 1925, Opel of Germany in 1929, and Australia's Holden's in 1931.

Sloan moved from president of GM to chairman in 1937, a post he held until 1956 when he became honourary chairman. During his lifetime he amassed a huge personal fortune, much of which he used to set up the Sloan Foundation, which established such organizations as the Sloan-Kettering Cancer Center.

Alfred P. Sloan, Jr., died at age 90 in the Sloan-Kettering Center in New York. Although it was the entrepreneurial spirit of Billy Durant that originally established General Motors, it was the administrative genius and vision of Alfred P. Sloan, Jr., that turned it into the world's mightiest manufacturing enterprise.

Robert Samuel McLaughlin

ROBERT SAMUEL MCLAUGHLIN: 1871 – 1972
GENERAL MOTORS OF CANADA

When John McLaughlin emigrated as a young man from County Tyrone in Ireland in 1832, and took up 160 acres of crown land in Ontario's Durham County six miles (10 km) north of Bowmanville, he was putting in motion a series of events that would have a significant impact on Canadian life. His grandson Robert Samuel McLaughlin would prove to be Canada's greatest motor vehicle manufacturer.

Other Irish immigrants settled in the area, and they named their little community Tyrone after their home county back in Ireland. John built a cabin, cleared the land, established a farm, married and raised a family, the eldest of whom was a boy named Robert.

The McLaughlins lived a typical thrifty rural Ontario life, producing almost everything they required right on the farm. There was little money for salt, sugar and tea, but they did manage to raise a small amount of cash from the sale of the potash that resulted from burning the trees as they cleared their land.

When Robert grew big enough to wield an axe, he too got into the tree cutting business. But he also took up a hobby that would eventually lead to a much larger enterprise.

Robert loved wood, whittling and shaping it at every opportunity, and began to occupy his spare time carving axe handles. He had a natural talent, and the handles he produced were so carefully crafted and exquisitely shaped that when his father took them to Bowmanville on market day, the merchants were willing to pay a premium price for the McLaughlin axe handles.

The immediate result was that this supplemented the small cash flow produced by the sale of potash. The much longer-term result was that those axe handles were, in a very real sense, the roots of the mighty General Motors of Canada motor manufacturing empire that we know today.

Robert went through the same cycle as his father had. When he married Mary Smith from nearby Enniskillen, his father gave him 50 acres of virgin forest to clear for a farm. He built a house and a driving shed with a big work bench in it where he continued to produce his fine axe handles. They were an important source of income while establishing the farm.

His love of woodworking was a strong as ever and he soon decided to try building a cutter based on pictures he had seen in an old catalogue. Robert naturally applied the same meticulous workmanship to it as he had to his axe handles.

While construction of the cutter was under way, a visiting neighbour was so impressed with it that he asked if he could buy it when it was completed. Robert said no, but that he would be glad to make him one just like it.

Thus the first two-vehicle "production line" began in a tiny driving shed in the community of Tyrone just north of Bowmanville. The year 1867 was to mark not only the beginning of a company, but also of a country, Canada.

Robert could make all of the wooden components of the cutter but he was at the mercy of the skilled tradesmen such as upholsterers and blacksmiths who journeyed from place to place (the origin of the term "journeyman" to describe a person with a skilled trade).

When the late arrival of the blacksmith jeopardized the sale of his first vehicle, Robert vowed not to be dependent on the itinerant blacksmith again. He established his own tiny blacksmith shop in front of his driving-shed-turned-factory.

Following the successful sale of his first vehicle, Robert added wagons to his line. Business flourished and within two years had outgrown the Tyrone building. He moved the operation to Enniskillen, where he built a two-storey building with a separate blacksmith shop.

With the new larger premises, Robert decided to try building a carriage. True to McLaughlin form, the fine craftsmanship on his phaeton won first prize at the Bowmanville fall fair against several established carriage makers. The die was cast; Robert immediately switched from wagons to carriages.

While Robert was building his business, he and Mary had also been busy having their family. Jack was born in 1866, George in 1869, and Robert Samuel in 1871. Unfortunately for the young family, Mary died in 1878, the year Robert moved the rapidly expanding operation to Oshawa.

Robert, or the "Governor" as his sons affectionately nicknamed him, continued to insist on top quality workmanship, with the result that the business expanded and its reputation grew.

But while he had control over the quality of the wood, paint and upholstery that went into his carriages, Robert wasn't satisfied with the type of metal undercarriages that were available. In the 1880s, therefore, he developed his own undercarriage, the most significant feature of which was a much superior "fifth wheel" steering mechanism.

McLaughlin had invented the new undercarriage for use in his own carriages. When a travelling salesman by the name of Tony Foster saw it, he told Robert that he was sure he could sell it to other carriage builders. Robert agreed, and the sale of undercarriages led to a large expansion of the business, particularly the blacksmith shop.

While the McLaughlin Carriage Co. was continuing to prosper and establish a national reputation, Robert's three sons were growing into their teen years. Jack attended the University of Toronto, graduated with a degree in chemistry, concocted a ginger flavoured soft drink, and went on to found an enterprise called the Canada Dry Co.

Sam was a bright student and graduated from high school at age 16. Both he and George joined the Governor in the carriage business, although they received no special treatment; they had to sweep the floor and do all of the mundane chores that are the lot of apprentices. Sam began his apprenticeship as an upholsterer in 1887.

Following completion of his three-year apprenticeship Sam became a journeyman upholsterer. He wanted to find out if he was skilled enough to make the full journeyman's rate of $1.75 per day in other high quality shops. This led him to New York state where he worked at several carriage companies, and did receive the full journeyman's rate.

Sam was now satisfied that his skills were among the best, so he took his bankroll and blew it on a fling in New York city. When he arrived back in Oshawa with 15 cents in his pocket Sam rejoined the family company, ready to settle down making carriages, or so he thought.

By 1890 the McLaughlin Carriage Co. of Oshawa was well established with a good reputation for quality products. The sale of Robert's running gear to other carriage makers soon formed an important part of the business, although high quality carriages and sleighs were still the company's main products.

Now back in the business, Sam was upholstery shop foreman for a couple of years, then started to take a more active role in the management of the business. Robert made Sam and George full partners in the company in 1892.

Sam had once thought he would like to be a draughtsman and had taken a correspondence course in drafting. The skill was soon put to good use when he began designing all of the company's products – no mean feat because by the turn of the century McLaughlin was offering 143 models of carriages and sleighs, with new models expected every year.

Sam took a fling at politics and was an Oshawa councillor for one term, but found that he didn't have the time for it. He married Adelaide Mowbray of Tyrone in 1898 and they produced a family of five daughters, one of whom, Isabel, became a highly acclaimed artist.

In December, 1899 disaster stuck when the plant was destroyed by fire. The future looked dark, but it quickly became apparent that the McLaughlins' reputation was solid; they received offers of assistance from 15 Ontario municipalities trying to entice them to relocate.

Oshawa, of course, didn't want to be out-done, and the McLaughlins accepted the town's offer of a $50,000 loan, to be repaid "as convenient." The new plant was ready for production by the next summer.

Shortly after the turn of the century the emerging automobile was turning out to be a craze, and companies were popping up like mushrooms to cash in on the demand. By 1905 the car was firmly established. Men such as Ransom Olds and Henry Ford in Michigan were successfully building and selling them.

This trend was not lost on Sam. Although he was able to convince his reluctant brother George that they should go into the car business, he was never able to convince the Governor that the automobile held a future for the McLaughlins. But to his credit, Robert did not stand in the way of Sam's drive to get the company into the car business; he just didn't have any interest in it.

Sam took a vacation and toured several American car factories to learn what was available, and how one went about getting into the automobile business. He finally settled on the Jackson car of Jackson, Michigan, as the vehicle they could assemble in Oshawa.

Fortunately, before making a final commitment, Sam and Oliver Hezzlewood, a McLaughlin executive, tested two of the Jacksons and found their performance sadly deficient. That spelled the end of the Jackson deal.

During his visit to Jackson, Sam encountered William C. "Billy" Durant, an old acquaintance and carriage maker from Flint, Michigan. They agreed that if the Jackson car deal fell through, Sam would discuss the matter with Durant, who had recently purchased the Buick Motor Co. of Flint.

When the Jackson deal failed, Sam didn't go immediately to see Durant. He was getting shrewder in this car business, and before talking to Billy, came back to Toronto and bought a new Buick to see if it was any good.

Sam was quickly convinced that the Buick with its reliable overhead valve engine was a quality product, and set up a meeting with Durant. Unfortunately, they couldn't agree on terms and no deal was struck, although McLaughlin and Durant parted good friends.

Now more than ever Sam was sure of the need to get into the car business, and convinced the company to design and build its own model. Arthur Milbrath, an engineer, was hired and by 1907 everything was in place to begin production. Unfortunately, Milbrath became seriously ill before production could begin and the project was in danger of foundering. Sam wired his old friend Durant to ask whether he could lend them an engineer until Milbrath recovered.

Durant, ever the entrepreneur, said he would be right over, and was in Oshawa the next day to

1922 McLaughlin, for a while they were McLaughlins, and then they became McLaughlin Buicks

of their vast experience in building carriages, would build the bodies. Sam was finally in the automobile business; 193 cars were produced in 1907.

The McLaughlin Motor Co. flourished in Canada. In the U.S. Durant founded the General Motors Co., later General Motors Corp. It took a financial interest in McLaughlin, and as president of the Canadian operation, Sam was made a vice-president of General Motors. The McLaughlins continued to make carriages and sleighs until 1915, when Sam sold that business to take on the manufacturing of Chevrolets, again in a deal with his old friend Durant. Shortly after that Chevrolet became part of General Motors when Durant used it to regain the control of GM that he had lost in 1910.

talk to Sam. But he didn't bring an engineer; rather, he brought two of his senior executives and this time they were able to make a deal. A 15 year contract was signed enabling McLaughlin to build Buicks, first called McLaughlins, but later when Buick became a famous U.S. make, McLaughlin-Buicks. They carried that name until 1942.

Durant would provide the engine and other mechanical parts and the McLaughlins, because

The end for the McLaughlin Motor Car Co. name came in 1918 when it was bought by General Motors (which already owned part of it) on the condition that Sam and George would stay on and run the business, which became General Motors of Canada. With the retirement of George from the vice-presidency in 1924, Sam became the last McLaughlin in the business that his father had started 57 years earlier in his driving shed.

Samuel McLaughlin in 1908 McLaughlin outside his beloved Parkwood home in Oshawa, Ontario

When George retired Sam decided to take it a little easier. He became chairman of the board of GM of Canada, while still remaining a vice-president of the U.S. parent organization. He retired in 1967, but remained honourary chairman of GM of Canada.

Sam McLaughlin never forgot his roots, nor his loyalty to Oshawa, which benefited greatly from "Mr. Sam's" philanthropy. The McLaughlin Planetarium in Toronto is another example of his generosity, and he was an active supporter of the Boy Scouts.

Robert Samuel McLaughlin lived in his beautiful and beloved Parkwood in Oshawa until the end. He died in his 101st year on January 6, 1972. He was one of Canada's true automotive pioneers.

An Overview of European and Asian Automotive History

The History to 1900:
The Foundation is Laid

North America adopted the automobile early in the 20th century as an instrument of affordable mass mobility, and created the production system to satisfy this demand. The evolution in Europe and Asia was different. For many years after its invention in Europe the automobile remained largely the preserve of the wealthy. In Japan there was no significant automobile production until after World War II, but when they did get under way they rose to be a world power in a relatively short time.

Europe, America and Asia, therefore, made contributions to the evolution of the automobile in different ways. The Europeans (Germany) invented it in the late 19th century, North America democratized it in the early 20th century, and Asia (Japan) pushed it to new levels of refinement in the late 20th century.

Prior to the automobile's roots, the credit for creating the world's first mechanically driven, self-propelled road vehicle is given to a Swiss engineer named Nicholas Cugnot who constructed a huge, three-wheeled, steam-driven artillery wagon in 1769. It was big and cumber-some, but it did move under its own power. Because it was steam powered, however, it was not the true geneses of the internal combustion engine driven automobile we know today. It is recorded here because it was the first self propelled vehicle.

The credit for inventing the practical internal combustion engine powered car is given to two Germans, Gottlieb Daimler and Karl Benz. Working independently, and located less than 100 kilometres (62 miles) apart, Daimler and Benz both developed self-propelled, engine-driven vehicles in 1885-86. Benz patented his rear-engined, three-wheeled "Patent Motorwagen" on January 29, 1886, and since his was the first such patent, he thus assumes the title of "Father of the Automobile."

Karl Benz, was born in November, 1844, and studied engineering at Karlsruhe Polyteknikum. While there he helped install a Lenoir gas engine in a factory in Stuttgart. It made a lasting impression. Upon graduation Benz worked in a variety of engineering jobs, including building steam engines, weigh scales, and bridges, but his interest

Karl Benz   *Gottlieb Daimler*

remained with the internal combustion engine. By 1871 he and a partner August Ritter were able to open a machine shop in Mannheim.

Ritter soon departed, but Benz persisted, eventually developing an internal combustion engine of his own design. He used benzine (gasoline) as a fuel, thereby freeing his engine from the city's illuminating gas supply lines. His first effort operated on the two-stroke principle, but with the apparently imminent demise of the 1877 Nicholas Otto patent on the four-stroke, he quietly switched to four strokes early in the 1880s. In 1883 Benz was able to establish Benz & Cie., in Mannheim to manufacture his engines.

Although his backers insisted that Benz concentrate on building stationary engines, he was able to work part-time on his secret ambition of motorizing a road vehicle. The machine that evolved in 1885 was a 263 kg (580 lb) three-wheeler with one wheel in front and two at the rear. It is said that Benz used three wheels because he didn't know how to make the steering gear for a four-wheeler.

The engine was mounted horizontally behind the seat, and the light framing and wheels were adapted from bicycle practice. An outstanding feature of Benz's engine was the use of a coil and battery ignition system, and a sparkplug which he had designed. It solved the vexing air-fuel mixture ignition problem that had been plaguing other engineers, including Daimler. Benz & Cie. would begin producing cars built to order in 1890.

Gottlieb Daimler was born in 1834, ten years earlier than Benz, and studied engineering at the

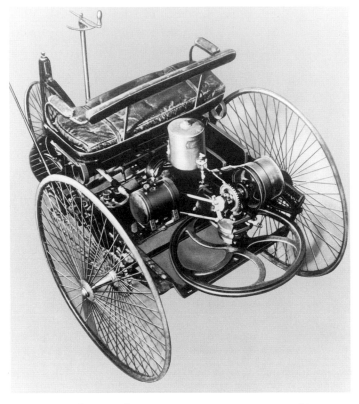

Karl Benz's first car, the "Patent Motorwagen" patented in 1886

Stuttgart Polyteknikum. He worked at various jobs, including making guns, and then steam engines. One of his positions was managing the Bruderhaus (Brother House) manufacturing facility located 35 kilometres (22 miles) south of Stuttgart.

Brother House was a shelter based on Christian principles that took care of orphaned and underprivileged boys, and included a light manufacturing plant where the boys were taught trades. Although Brother House may not have been one of Daimler's highest profile positions, it did bring him into contact with a person who would play a significant role in his life. While Daimler was there he met Wilhelm Maybach, a student who impressed him deeply with his keen intelligence and hard work. Maybach and Daimler formed a bond that would last a lifetime, and Maybach would go on to become a brilliant engineer.

Daimler became interested in the emerging internal combustion engine, which he learned about on a visit to Paris. There, Jean-Joseph Etienne Lenoir was manufacturing a coal gas fuelled engine he had developed.

Lenoir's engine had been an inspiration to a German named Nicholas August Otto. Otto and partner Eugen Langen developed a more efficient version of Lenoir's engine, which they showed at the 1867 Paris Exposition. It was awarded a gold medal. The ensuing good publicity enabled them to combine Otto's engineering skill with Langen's resources to form a Cologne-based company called Gasmotorenfabrik Deutz to manufacture their new engine.

Gasmotorenfabrik Deutz flourished, but the partners' management abilities didn't match their technical expertise, with the result that they were soon away behind in filling orders. Needing a good production manager to run the business, they engaged Gottlieb Daimler in 1872. He soon hired his former student Wilhelm Maybach as chief design engineer.

Although Gasmotorenfabrik was successful, their engine was still crude. It operated on the atmospheric principle, and this lack of internal compression of the air-fuel mixture made it very inefficient. An American inventor named George Brayton had developed a more efficient system in which the mixture was compressed in one cylinder and burned in another.

Faced with this competition, Otto began work on a new engine, and by 1876 had developed one using the four stroke principle, one for each upward and downward movement of the piston during two crankshaft revolutions. These four cycles were: intake, the ingestion of air/fuel mixture as the piston descended; compression, the squeezing of the mixture as the piston ascended; power, the pressure and expansion as the ignited mixture burned and pushed the piston down; and exhaust, the expelling of the burned gases as the piston ascended to begin the four cycles all over again. A heavy flywheel fitted to the crankshaft provided the inertia to keep the cycles continuing.

Two-stroke engines would continue to be used – Otto and Langen's early engine was, as noted, a two-stroke – often with supercharging, or by compressing the mixture in the engine's crankcase to accomplish the four cycles in two piston strokes, or one crankshaft revolution. But four-stroke engines would prevail, and it was Otto's four-stroke principle that really gained popularity and laid the groundwork for the development of the self propelled, internal combustion engine powered car.

The "Otto-cycle" engine was patented on August 4, 1877. The patent would later be voided, based on the discovery of an earlier four-stroke cycle patent granted to Frenchman Alphonse Beau de Rochas in 1861 (although he apparently never built an engine). In spite of this, Otto's patent would ensure that his name was forever associated with the four-stroke internal combustion engine.

While Otto was developing his new engine, the industrious Daimler was increasing the company's production. But in spite of this prosperity, Daimler and Otto were continually in disagreement. One of their sources of difference was Daimler's interest in changing their engines' fuel from town gas, which tied them to one location, to benzine.

Benzine was a plentiful waste product that resulted from the distillation of the crude oil being pumped from the many oil wells being discovered in North America and Russia during the past 20 years. Daimler believed that an engine thus liberated had greatly expanded potential. A showdown inevitably came, and Langen had to make a choice between keeping Otto or Daimler. Since the patent was in Otto's name, Daimler was let go.

Gottlieb Daimler's first car, 1886

Daimler's time with Gasmotorenfabrik had left him far from destitute. He was able to buy a large house in Cannstatt, near Stuttgart, where his wife Emma wanted him to retire. While his family loved the house, what really excited Daimler was a big greenhouse on the property. Retirement was far from his mind. He turned the greenhouse into a shop and invited his old friend Wilhelm Maybach to leave Deutz Gasmotorenfabrik and join him. The two mechanical geniuses were back together, and both were obsessed with the idea of developing an internal combustion engine that was better than anyone had ever built before.

Daimler's vision of a better engine lay in making one that was smaller, lighter, and ran at a higher speed. Daimler and Maybach laboured in their converted greenhouse, and eventually constructed an internal combustion four-stroke engine that weighed 45 kg (100 lb), compared with Otto's 340 (750). And while the Otto turned only some 180 revolutions per minute, the Daimler-Maybach design reached the unprecedented speed of 900 rpm. They had some concern about Otto's four-stroke patent, but it was then under attack, and it was becoming apparent that it may soon be rescinded. This did occur in 1886 when Beau de Roches's earlier patent was uncovered, thereby releasing the four-stroke principle to all who wished to pursue it.

With the Daimler high-speed, benzine-burning engine, it was a relatively short step to a motorized vehicle. They first tried their engine on a motorcycle, and then used it to power a boat. Following this came their four-wheeled motorized carriage in 1886. Daimler Motoren-Gesellschaft would be formed in 1890 in Bad Cannstatt to produce Daimler cars.

Thus evolved the forerunner of the modern automobile. Although many engineers contributed to the development of better engines, it was Karl Benz, Gottlieb Daimler and Wilhelm Maybach who would bring the road vehicle and the engine together and create a successful automobile.

Others followed the lead of Daimler and Benz. France adopted the new motor car with enthusiasm, and would soon surge ahead of Germany in production. The rights to the Daimler engine were purchased by Edouard Sarazin for wood-working machinery manufacturers Perrin, Panhard and Cie of France in 1887. Mr. Sarazin died shortly thereafter, and his widow married Emile Levassor, which under French law passed the engine rights to Mr. Levassor.

Levassor and Rene Panhard joined forces, and in 1891 they introduced their Panhard-Levassor car which pointed the way to what would become the standard automobile layout. The engine was mounted in the front, the gear-box was in the middle, and the drive, although by chains rather than a shaft, went to the rear wheels. Other French firms also adopted the Daimler engine.

It should be noted that in the early days of the automobile steam and electric powered vehicles were also part of the emerging automotive scene. Steamers benefitted from their already long period of development. They were fast and powerful, but suffered the disadvantages of being heavy, taking time to get up steam, and requiring a skilled operator.

Electric cars were quiet and easy to drive, and commanded a share of the market. Disadvantages were that they needed to carry a heavy battery load and had a limited driving range, making them essentially urban vehicles. Electrics did set the world's land speed record when it was first established in 1898, and held it until 1902, but

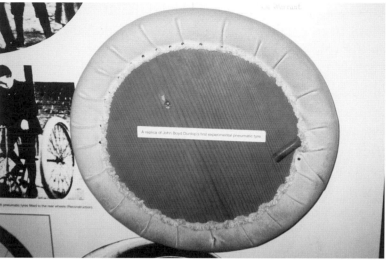

Replica of John Dunlop's first 1888 pneumatic tire

lost the title to steam. Steam cars were soon vanquished by internal combustion engined cars, which would hold the record from then on.

The solid wheels used on carriages, buggies and bicycles gave an uncomfortable, bone-shaking ride, and were not suitable for high road speeds. Thus, a development that would have great significance for the automobile was the 1888 invention of the pneumatic tire by an Irish veterinarian named John Dunlop. "Re-invented" would really be a better term because a patent had been taken out for a pneumatic tire in 1845 by an Englishman named Robert William Thomson. But there was apparently little interest in Thomson's tire, and it languished into oblivion. Dr. Dunlop was almost certainly unaware of the

Thomson patent when he created the first pneumatic tire by taping rubber tubes to his son's tricycle wheels to reduce the road vibration.

The Peugeot family of France, manufacturers of such products as tools and coffee mills, came on the automobile scene early. After experimenting with steam powered cars starting in 1889, they soon switched to Daimler's gasoline engine. Peugoet was selling gasoline powered cars to the public by 1891, and would later pioneer the twin overhead camshaft, four-valves-per-cylinder engine that appeared in its 1912 Grand Prix racer.

Four-valve cylinders would become the standard of the racing world. In road cars they would be pretty well limited to such exotic cars as the Duesenberg and Stutz until the 1980s, when they would proliferate in production cars as engineers strove for more power from smaller engines.

The Automobile Club of France organized the first official automobile road race, the Paris-Bordeaux-Paris, in 1895. France's lead in auto racing led to French being adopted as the official language of racing. The Paris-Bordeaux-Paris was a significant event because it began the European trend to open road races that would last until the 1950s. This, along with the demanding terrain and crowded conditions in much of Europe, placed a premium on good roadholding. European cars, therefore, would evolve with suspensions, brakes, steering and tires that generally provided cornering, control and braking superior to those of North American cars.

Automobile racing would soon be legislated off the public roads in North America, and onto closed oval tracks. This, plus the wide expanses of level terrain would produce an entirely different type of car in America, one that emphasized a soft, quiet ride.

While Europe was concentrating on developing good handling cars, as the automobile matured America would concentrate on such comfort and convenience features as the fully automatic transmission, soft "cushion-ride" tires, and air conditioning. And because gasoline was much cheaper in the New World, North American cars would grow larger and heavier than most of those produced in Europe, and be powered by engines that were bigger, thirstier and less efficient.

With all of the pioneering activity taking place on the Continent in the late 19th century, little automotive development was occurring in England, in spite of its advanced machine tool industry. Much of the blame can be laid at the feet of the Locomotives on Highways Act passed in 1865 to retard the development of steam-powered road vehicles.

Commonly called the "Red Flag Law," it required a person to walk in front of a motor vehicle, and to carry a red flag during the day and a lantern at night. It limited speed to four miles per hour, and stayed in effect until 1896, thwarting Britain's development of powered road vehicles for more than 30 years. It was rescinded in 1896, and British motorists celebrated the occasion with the London-to-Brighton run, an event that is still carried out today with cars of the same vintage as originally used.

With the yoke of the Red Flag Law lifted, Britain quickly began developing a motor industry. The Daimler Motor Syndicate was formed to import Daimler cars in 1896, and would soon develop cars of its own design as it became separate from the German firm.

A significant French company of the period was de Dion-Bouton, formed in 1883 by Count Albert de Dion, George Bouton and Charles Trepardoux to produce heavy commercial vehicles. They also produced a steam-powered tricycle, and the Count was soon experimenting with gasoline engines, so upsetting Trepardoux that he left the company. In addition to his internal combustion engine experiments, de Dion would develop a form of rear suspension in which the wheels were secured by a solid axle, while the power was transmitted to the wheels by articulated half-shafts extending from a frame-mounted differential. It would be used right

1898 DeDion-Bouton

up to the modern era.

Building on the pioneering efforts of Daimler and Benz, de Dion-Bouton developed a 137 cc single cylinder, air cooled engine that could reach higher revolutions per minute than the German engines. This was due to the invention of an electric ignition distributor with a revolving commutator that opened and closed the primary circuit at precise intervals. This sent a coil-induced spark across the spark plug electrodes, igniting the air-fuel mixture in the cylinder at exactly the right time. It was a breakthrough that predicted the ignition systems used in cars until the advent of electronic spark control in the 1970s. The de Dion-Bouton ignition system was patented in 1895.

The little de Dion-Bouton engine could be increased from 1/2 to 12 horsepower or more by enlarging its displacement and running it at higher rpm. The company applied its high speed engine to three-and four-wheeled vehicles. The de Dion-Bouton engine became an important building block of the automobile industry, and was soon being used by some 140 automobile manufacturers, including France's Delage, founded in 1894, and Renault, founded in 1898. Both went on to become prominent French auto manufacturers.

1900 TO WORLD WAR II: AUTOMOBILE MANUFACTURING PROLIFERATES

With Germany and France having put the building blocks in place for the development of the automobile, and England's Red Flag Law having been defeated, the progress of the car proceeded apace. The Wolseley Sheep Shearing Machine Co. of Birmingham, England decided to go into the automobile business. Its general manager, Herbert Austin, produced the first Wolseley, and left in 1906 to establish his own Austin Motor Co. It would become one of Britain's greatest auto producers. The Singer Co., a bicycle manufacturer in Coventry, began building cars in 1905. By the late 1920s Singer would stand third in sales behind Morris and Austin.

In Sweden, the Scania bicycle company began building cars in Malmo in about 1902. Minerva of Belgium, builders of bicycles and motorcycles, went into automobile production in 1904, and would later produce some of Europe's mightiest motorcars.

The form of the automobile was gradually evolving from its wagon and carriage roots. Engines were moving from under or behind the seat to a position in front of the driver, with a shaft taking the drive to the rear wheels. Tillers were being replaced by steering wheels.

The car that really solidified the layout of the automobile was the 1901 Mercedes 35PS Touring. It was manufactured by Daimler Motoren Gasellschaft, and it was named after Mercedes Jellinek, the daughter of Emil Jellinek, a self-appointed, unofficial, later official, Daimler distributor in the resort town of Nice, France.

After purchasing several Daimler cars, the dashing Jellinek decided that he needed a much faster one, and asked Daimler to build it for him. To add weight to his request, he placed an order for 36 cars with the stipulation that they be named after his daughter Mercedes. It was an offer that Daimler could not afford to refuse. Gottlieb Daimler had died in 1900, so the design of the car fell to Wilhelm Maybach and Gottlieb Daimler's son Paul.

The first car to bear the Mercedes name owed nothing to the carriage and bicycle technology that had inspired so many previous automobiles. It had its engine in front, and was fitted with a gated four-speed transmission. At only 998 kg (2200 lb), and

1902 Mercedes, standardizing the layout

with 35 horsepower, it could reach 88 km/h (55 mph), and was victorious in all of its trials at the famous Nice Week in 1901. It established Mercedes as the name to be reckoned with in automobiles.

The British auto industry was now up and running, and was not to be denied. Frederick Lanchester's Lanchester Engine Co. produced its first production car in 1900, an imaginative design that drew little from previous practice. It was England's first truly practical car, and it was marvellously engineered. The centrally positioned, horizontally-opposed twin cylinder engine had separate, counter-rotating crankshafts for each cylinder, thereby cancelling out vibration and making it extremely smooth running for that period.

England's famous Rolls-Royce was the result of a meeting between Henry Royce, a meticulous manufacturer of electrical/mechanical equipment in Manchester, and Charles Rolls, an extroverted Panhard agent in London who wanted a quality British car to sell. After experimenting with several models, they evolved the Silver Ghost in 1907, which would be produced until 1925. It proved so durable and trouble-free that it led to Rolls-Royce's claim, with justification, that it built the best car in the world.

The Hillman-Coatalen Motor Car Co., soon the Hillman Motor Car Co., was formed in Coventry in 1907. They produced a line of sturdy if conventional cars that enabled them to become one of Britain's well respected car makers. It became part of super salesman William Rootes's Rootes Group of companies in 1928.

Vauxhall Iron Works of London began producing cars in 1904, and would build a solid reputation for both sporty and family vehicles. It would be acquired by General Motors Corp. in 1925, and became GM's British operation. GM would not limit its off-shore acquisitions to Britain. In the late 1920s it acquired Germany's Adam Opel, and would establish General Motors' Holden's in Australia, which manufactured an all-Australian car following World War II.

Ford Motor Co. had also set up a British operation in 1911 to manufacture right-hand drive versions of the famous Model T and A, before

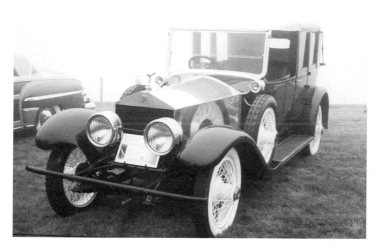

1923 Rolls-Royce Silver Ghost, established the mystique

1939 Jaguar SS100 3.5 L, pre-WWII performance car

changing to cars of English design. Ford would bring its moving auto assembly line to Britain.

The Standard Motor Co. was established in Coventry in 1903 by an entrepreneur named R.W. Maudslay. It began modestly with a one cylinder car that had its engine under the seat, but soon progressed to conventional layouts. By offering good value for money it soon numbered among Britain's leading car makers.

In 1932, William Lyons, who had started out with partner William Walmsley making Zeppelin-shaped motorcycle side-cars in his Blackpool garage in 1922, and later customized such cars as Austin Sevens, took the full step into car building using Standard chassis.

Lyons would form his own company, S.S. Cars

Ltd., in 1934, and it would build its first Jaguar badged car in 1936. The company was changed to Jaguar Cars Ltd. in 1945, the S.S. name having acquired negative connotations during World War II. Jaguar would continue to rely on Standard for its engines until it was able to develop its own, the fabulous double overhead cam six that appeared in the equally fabulous 1949 Jaguar XK120 roadster.

William R. Morris, later Lord Nuffield, an Oxford automobile dealer, decided to produce his own light car, the Morris Oxford in 1913. It was a successful enterprise, and out of it would also flow the famous MG (for Morris Garages) sports car that dominated small displacement racing in the 1930s, and went on to initiate the sports car movement in North America following World War II.

Up in Bradford, Yorkshire, the Jowett brothers Benjamin and William, bicycle mechanics, formed Jowett Motor Manufacturing to build engines, and by 1913 were marketing their own car. Jowetts featured horizontally-opposed two cylinder engines, until a flat four was added in 1936. Jowetts were particularly noted for their fuel economy, and carved out a solid niche in the marketplace.

Another marketplace niche was filled by three-wheeled cars. They got a sales boost in Britain for many years because they were taxed at the same rate as motorcycles, provided they weighed less than eight hundredweight, or 406 kg (896 lb). This gave them a distinct advantage over such four-wheeled small cars as the Austin Seven and the first Morris Minor.

Although several companies sold three-wheelers in Britain and other countries, the most famous was the Morgan which H.F.S. Morgan produced from 1910 to 1950. Morgan is still in business producing 10 of its anachronistic, four-wheeled sports cars per week in the classic fashion at Malvern Link, Worcester.

Walter Owen Bentley, known as "W.O.," already successful as a car importer, designer of rotary aero engines, and tireless promoter of the aluminum piston, decided to produce his own car. He established Bentley Motors Ltd., in London in 1920, and began the production of cars with powerful, long-stroke, overhead cam engines. They soon developed a reputation for speed, particularly in long distance races, and from 1924 to 1930 would bring England five wins in the famous LeMans, France, 24-hour endurance race, a feat not repeated by Britain until Jaguar did it in the 1950s.

Bentleys were large, rugged cars, the most famous and impressive of which was the 4-1/2 litre Black Label with its big, Roots-type supercharger mounted between the dumb-irons in front of the radiator. The company fell into receivership in 1931, and was taken over by Rolls-Royce, following which Bentleys would become badge-engineered Rolls-Royces.

Although Britain had been slow entering the automobile industry in the beginning, it quickly picked up momentum. By 1932 it was Europe's largest auto manufacturer, and second in the world only to the U.S. At the end of the 1930s British car production would be dominated by six companies: Morris, Austin, Ford, Vauxhall, Rootes, and Standard.

In Italy, the Anonima Lombarda Fabbrica Automobili (Lombardy Motor Manufacturing Co.), or ALFA, was formed in 1909 when several businessmen took over the failing French Darracq plant in Portello, near Milan. They produced their first Alfa car in 1911, and went on to produce a variety of medium sized and large models. Italy's terrain demanded cars with good brakes and a favourable power-to-weight ratio, which made Alfas ideally suited for competition. Recognizing the value of competition, both for development and publicity, Alfa became active in racing.

In 1915 ALFA was taken over by an industrialist named Nicola Romeo, and following World War I, the cars became known as Alfa Romeos. The company built both road and competition models, and would distinguish itself as one of the most successful Italian racing marques in history. Notable was the P3 Grand Prix car of the 1930s. It was powered by a twin overhead camshaft, supercharged straight-eight engine, and was almost invincible for several years. Alfa Romeo transferred knowledge gained in Grand Prix racing to its road cars, which distinguished themselves in sports car competition. Alfa came under Fiat's control in 1987, and continues to produce highly respected cars.

Another significant Italian automobile company was formed early. Fabbrica Italiana Automobili Torino, or Fiat, an industrial giant which also manufactured such products as commercial vehicles, ships and aero and marine engines, began building cars at the turn of the century. It produced a variety of car sizes, including a large V-12. It even set up the Fiat Automobile Co. in Poughkeepsie, New York, in 1910 to build and market its cars. This facility continued Fiat production until 1918.

1937 Fiat Topolino, Italy's "People's Car"

One of Fiat's most famous cars was the tiny Topolino (little mouse), introduced in 1936. It was Italy's version of the "People's Car." It accommodated two passengers, and was powered by a 570 cc four cylinder engine. Production would continue until 1948.

Fiat produced a staggering array of models over the years, and became Italy's predominant car maker. Fiats or their derivatives were produced in more than 20 counties. Although imported to North America for many years, Fiat didn't enjoy the New World sales success of the German or Japanese cars, although it did create a enthusiastic niche market.

One of Fiat's racing drivers, Vincenzo Lancia, was a man of innate technical prowess. He and

1922 Lancia Lambda, technical sophistication

partner Claudio Fogolin, also of Fiat, decided to go into automobile manufacturing. They set up Fabbrica Automobili Lancia in Turin in 1906 and had their first car ready by 1907. Lancias would prove to be technically advanced, having, for example, shaft drive when chains were still common, and being powered by engines of high speed for the era.

In 1922 the Lancia Lambda (Lancia's models were named after the Greek alphabet for many years, and then after old Roman highways), pioneered unit construction in which the frame and body are integrated into one unit. Also at this time Lancia introduced an advanced type of independent suspension in which the steering kingpins, also called sliding pillars, moved up and down supported by coil springs. It would prove so effective that Lancia would continue to use it until 1963. A similar principle is still employed by the English Morgan.

Always ready to swim out of the mainstream, in 1937 Lancia introduced the Aprilia with independent rear suspension via torsion bars. Its body was of efficient aerodynamic shape, and it had pillarless design so that when the front and rear doors were open there was completely unimpeded access to the interior. It remained in production until 1950.

Lancia had long used vee-type engines with very narrow angles between the cylinder banks - 10 to 14 degrees being typical -and with one cylinder head topping both banks. Then in 1950 the beautiful little Lancia Aurelia two-door sedan was introduced with what was for them a very wide-angle vee-type engine. This was a 60 degree V-6, the first V-6 to be offered in a production car.

Lancia would also excel in competition, both racing and rallying, for a period. The pressure of competition caught up with Lancia, however, and in 1969 it was forced to sell out to Fiat.

Another aspect of the Italian industry that must be acknowledged is styling. Not surprisingly, given Italy's history in the arts, Italian automobile stylists are recognized as the best. Men like Giorgetto Giugaro and Pinanfarina are among the world's finest car designers.

Although The Netherlands did not become

known as a great automobile nation, it did produce some significant firsts. Carriage makers Hendrik and Jacobus Spijker of Amsterdam began importing Benz cars in 1895, and started modifying them for their conditions. By 1900 they had produced their own Spyker car (the name was modified to facilitate exporting). Their first cars were fairly conventional for the time, although they were early in the use of shaft drive and a five-bearing crankshaft in a four cylinder engine.

Then in 1903 a Spyker appeared with a huge 8.5 litre six cylinder engine, said to be the first production six ever offered. In addition, it had four-wheel drive and four wheel brakes, both almost unheard of features at that time. The Spyker did not persist with four-wheel drive, but did produce a variety of models, all of which has some advanced features, such as its "dustless" undercarriage shrouding, and laterally positioned camshafts. The Spyker car was a favourite of Queen Wilhelmina of Holland. Alas, low sales brought Spyker production to an end in 1925.

Another much later Dutch effort at car building was the DAF, produced by Van Doornes Automobielfabriek of Eindhoven, a commercial vehicle manufacturer. Introduced in 1958, the little DAF Daffodil two-door sedan was powered by a 600 cc flat, two-cylinder, air cooled front-mounted engine.

By far the most interesting feature of the Daffodil was its rear-mounted, infinitely variable, "Variomatic" transmission. Using two wide rubber drive-belts, and four pulleys whose diameters could be varied by such mechanisms as engine torque, spring pressure, vacuum chambers and centrifugal weights, the effective gear ratio varied between 14.22:1 and 3.60:1 to meet the required wide range of operating conditions. It was a sound system that would be manufactured for many years.

At the dawn of the 20th century Japan was still a largely agrarian economy, but small stirrings of automobile interest began early. The first Japanese gasoline powered car, the Takuri, appeared in 1907, and 12 were built. It was a fine, sturdy car based on Western technology, but Takuri then abandoned its car-building efforts.

In 1910 the Tokyo Kunisue Automobile Works produced a limited number of small, four seaters, as well as a larger luxury sedan with a four cylinder engine. In 1911 Masuijiro Hashimoto formed the Kwaishinsha Motor Car Co., and in 1916 produced a significant model which was called the DAT. It was the forerunner of the modern Datsun.

American William Gorham, after a failed attempt to establish an aeronautical company in Japan, set up the Jitsuyo Jidosha Co., and began producing a car called the Lila in 1919. After the Great Kanto Earthquake in 1923, Kwaishinsha and Jitsuyo joined in what would eventually become the Nissan Motor Co. Mitsubishi Heavy

1927 Bugatti Type 35, consolidated Bugatti's racing reputation

Industries also produced a limited number of cars from 1917 to 1921.

Although Japanese car production still numbered in the hundreds rather than the thousands, and most of the cars sold in Japan were imports, the foundations were already being laid for some of the automobile companies that would flourish following World War II.

In Europe, more auto manufacturers were being established. An Italian born engineer by the name of Ettore Bugatti moved to France, and after employment with several auto manufacturers, by 1910 was able to obtain the financial backing to open his own car company in Molsheim in the Department of Bas-Rhin. His cars were intricately engineered, and quickly proved themselves in competition. Bugatti built both road cars and race cars, and many of them, particularly the little Type 35, would become extremely successful in competition, rivalling the record of that later Italian entrepreneur, Enzo Ferrari.

Bugatti also produced one of the world's mightiest cars, the Type 41 Bugatti Royale, intended for royalty. It was a huge car powered by a 12.7 litre, overhead cam straight-eight engine that would later be used to power rail cars. Alas, the Royale appeared at the end of the 1920s, and was doomed by the Depression. Only six were built, and ironically, no royalty ever bought one. Bugattis were built until World War II, and although attempts were made to revive the name after the war, none was successful.

Bugatti was not the only company to offer large, luxury cars during the 1930s. It was similar to the story in America, where huge cars like the Duesenberg, Cadillac V-12 and V-16, Marmon, Lincoln and Packard, which had been conceived in the 1920s, came to market in the Depression of the 1930s.

In Europe such companies as Minerva of Belgium, Daimler-Benz, Horch and Maybach of Germany (the Maybach was created by Wilhelm Maybach's son Karl, also famous for his Zeppelin airship engines), Rolls-Royce of Britain, Hispano-Suiza of Spain, and Isotta-Fraschini of Italy built huge cars in the classic mode. Unfortunately very few people could afford to buy them, and those who could often didn't. Those monuments to ostentation were eerily out of step with the period.

Austin Seven, economical, affordable transportation

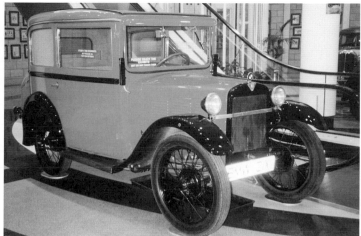

1931 BMW Dixi, from little acorns...

Another aspect of automobile engineering was starting to gain attention in Germany. This was aerodynamics, then often referred to as streamlining. Although its importance had been recognized many years earlier, it would not be fully appreciated for several decades more. Men such as Wunnibald Kamm, Edmund Rumpler and Paul Jaray laid down aerodynamic tenets that would form the basis for much future work in this area.

In England, the Austin Motor Co. had been initially successful, but found itself in receivership following World War I. It would recover with its durable Model 12, but Herbert Austin realized that a more affordable car was required, and introduced the tiny Austin Seven in 1922. It was powered by a 747 cc, four cylinder engine, and was to Britain what the Ford Model T was to

North America: an affordable, economical car that almost everyone could buy.

Although others such as Morris, Singer and Peugeot also produced baby cars, the Austin Seven was the most famous. It was an outstanding success, and was produced until 1938. It would also be built under licence as the Rosengart in France, the American Austin/ Bantam in the U.S., the Datsun in Japan, and the BMW Dixi in Germany.

Indeed it was the Dixi that gave Bayerische Motoren-Werke, famous for its airplane engines, its start in the automobile business. BMW's cars would flourish in the 1930s, its advanced 327 and 328 models with their hemispherical combustion chamber engines being notable. But to survive following World War II BMW would be forced to produce a car as humble as the Isetta bubblecar. But survive it did, and based largely on the popularity of its small 2002 sports sedan of the late 1960s and '70s, went on to rank among the world's greatest automobile manufacturers.

Although Scania-Vabis, and Thulin, had produced cars in Sweden, they had done so only in limited numbers. Sweden's auto industry was really established in 1927 when two employees of the Svenska Kullagerfabriken (SKF) bearing company, Gustaf Larson, an engineer, and Assar Gabrielsson, an economist, decided that Sweden should have its own car. With Gabrielsson attending to the financing of the enterprise, and Larson taking car of the engineering design, the first car, called the Volvo, for "I roll," was introduced in 1927. It was financially backed by SKF. Volvo would establish a reputation for sturdy, reliable cars, and would take a leading role in automobile safety. In 1959, for example, Volvo introduced the now universal three-point seat belt.

In France, André Citroen, the former chief engineer of Mors Automobiles of Paris, formed his own gear-making company in 1913, and in 1919 began manufacturing automobiles. Citroen developed a good reputation, and soon joined Peugeot and Renault as one of France's Big Three automakers. Citroen's advanced front-wheel drive Traction Avant model, introduced in 1934, did a great deal to popularize front drive, and would be made until 1955.

The two names that pioneered the automobile finally came together in 1926 when the Daimler and Benz companies joined to form Daimler Benz AG. Their cars would be called Mercedes-Benzes from then on, and as befits their founders, Mercedes-Benzes were always among the finest cars produced. The company would excel in both road and competition cars, and would continue as Daimler Benz until 1998 when M-B merged with America's Chrysler Corp. to become DaimlerChrysler.

All car companies suffered during the Depression of the 1930s. This led to failures and consolidations. In Germany, four manufacturers, Audi, DKW, Horch and Wanderer, came together under the Auto Union banner. DKW concentrated on two-stroke engines, and in 1931 had introduced a very advanced small car, the F1, also called the Front. By having its transversely-mounted front engine driving the front wheels, it anticipated by 28 years the British Motors Corp. Austin/Morris Mini that would set in motion the modern trend in cross-engine, front drive layouts.

When Adolf Hitler became chancellor of Germany in 1933 it was to have long term implications for the automobile world. An admirer of Henry Ford and what he had accomplished in transportation for the masses, Hitler was determined to have a German "People's Car" developed. For this he commissioned Ferdinand Porsche's Design Office in Stuttgart.

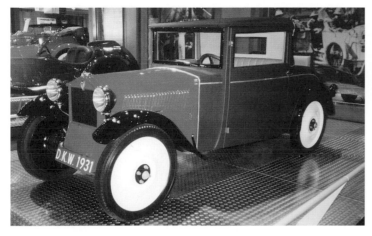

1931 DKW Front, early front-drive, cross-engine layout

1935 Volkswagen Prototype Beetle, modest beginnings

Ferdinand Porsche, along with pioneering engineer Hans Ledwinka, designer of the Czechoslovakian Tatra car, was a strong proponent of rear engine placement. Thus it was not surprising that he and his engineers produced a small, beetle-shaped sedan with a horizontally-opposed, air cooled, four cylinder engine located behind the rear axle. Three prototypes were built, and by 1936 rigorous testing proved the design to be sound. Hitler wanted the car to be called the Kraft Durch Freude (Strength Through Joy), but public opinion prevailed and it became the Volkswagen (People's Car).

When established German automakers showed little enthusiasm for building the Volkswagen, Hitler had a huge state-owned factory constructed approximately 80 kilometres (50 miles) east of Hanover near Wolfsburg Castle in the State of Lower Saxony. The Volkswagenwerk was completed in 1938, but would produce few Volkswagen cars. By this time Hitler's plans were far more sinister than building a car for the people, and the Wolfsburg plant would begin manufacturing a Volkswagen-based, Jeep-type military vehicle called the Kubelwagen, which also came in an amphibious "Schwimmwagen" version.

WORLD WAR II TO THE PRESENT: EUROPE RECOVERS; ASIA RISES

World War II was a watershed for society, and for the automobile industry. For the first time it would cease making cars, and turn its vast expertise and production capacity to making war materiel. With the war over in 1945, all companies began returning their factories to automobile production. For the victorious nations, it was relatively easy, but for the vanquished it was a prodigious task because of the war-time damage to their plants.

When the partition of East and West took place, several European companies, such as BMW and Auto Union, found their plants on the Communist side of the Iron Curtain. BMW lost its Eisenach factory, but still had its motorcycle facility in Munich. It began preparing that plant for car production, and the first Munich cars were produced in 1952.

The giant Volkswagenwerk was badly bomb-damaged, and fell under the control of the British after the war. They were sympathetic to the displaced persons and ex-prisoners of war who began returning to the hulking skeleton, and encouraged them in their quest to rebuild the plant. The British arranged for coal and steel to be shipped in, and a small number of Volkswagen Beetles began coming out of the factory, a total of 1785 in 1945, rising to 10,020 in 1946.

Volkswagenwerk really came to life in 1948 when Heinz Nordhoff, an ex-Opel engineer, took over the management of the company. He was hard-working and dedicated, and under his stewardship Volkswagen, with the aid of American Marshall Plan financing, would perform what was often referred to as a "Post-War Miracle."

The first Volkswagens were exported to America in 1949, and to Canada in 1952. The Volkswagen Beetle would go on to become the single most successful model in the world, surpassing the Ford Model T's 15,007,033 production total in February 1972. The original Beetles are still being built in Mexico, and total production has surpassed 22 million.

Volkswagen would also create its Transporter/Microbus series, which it introduced in 1950. It was the original minivan, a "box-on-wheels," the most space efficient people and cargo package for a given overall length. It used the Beetle sedan

1949 Volkswagen Beetle, begins its world domination

1961 Volkswagen Westfalia camper van, the original minivan

powertrain with reduction gears in the hubs to make it suitable for commercial use.

Transporter/Microbus competitors such as the DKW Karavan and the Fiat Multipla would arrive from European manufacturers in the 1950s. And in North America, the Volkswagen-knockoff Chevrolet rear engined Corvair Greenbrier, plus Ford's Econoline and Dodge's D-100, came in the 1960s. But they would fade away, and Volkswagen would have the minivan field pretty much to itself again until Chrysler's Dodge Caravan and Plymouth Voyager arrived in 1984. In spite of Chrysler's claims, it didn't invent the minivan, although it certainly can take credit for bringing it into the mainstream of the automotive world.

As in North America, after World War II the established European auto manufacturers re-

turned to building warmed over versions of pre-war models until they could design new ones. With the pent-up demand for new cars that was left over from the Depression and the war, manufacturers could sell all the cars they could produce. This would allow companies that had been performing marginally before the war to hang on a little longer. But when the market returned to normal, consolidation would begin.

This period would also entice new entrepreneurs to enter the market. Sweden would get its second car company when aircraft manufacturer Svenska Aeroplan AB (SAAB) decided to start building a kind of "Swedish Volkswagen." It designed a small, aerodynamic, front-wheel drive sedan, initially using a pre-war DKW, two-stroke, two cylinder engine and transmission. The engine was mounted transversely, and drove the front wheels. Saab would remain faithful to its front-drive configuration.

The Saab 92 was announced to the press in 1947, but production didn't get under way until 1950. Saab would later move to a two-stroke, three cylinder engine, and then to four-stroke fours. The Saab, although always somewhat quirky and out of the mainstream, would nevertheless build a good reputation and a solid following.

In Germany, Ferdinand Porsche of Volkswagen fame, and his son Ferdinand (Ferry), also an engineer, conceived a two seater sports car based on Volkswagen components. This model 356, as it was called, used a slightly modified Volkswagen platform and driveline clothed in low, aerody-

1948 Porsche 356 number one, sleek lines belie modest Volkswagen Beetle heritage

namic coachwork. The first prototype was ready by 1948. Production gradually increased, and the 356, like the Volkswagen, would prove extremely robust. It demonstrated its durability and speed by winning its class at LeMans on is first try in 1951, the beginning of Porsche's long and illustrious competition career.

Porsche would gradually evolve away from the use of Volkswagen components, but would, except for a period in the 1970s and '80s, stay faithful to horizontally-opposed engines located in the rear. It would even retain air cooling until forced to go to water cooled engines for power, emissions and noise reasons in the 1990s.

Enzo Ferrari in Italy, who had managed Alfa Romeo's racing team in the 1930s, decided to

1950 Saab 92, aircraft maker turns to cars

1950 Ferrari 166, twelve cylinder exotica

Minx, and smaller makers such as Jowett and Singer produced new models which were strongly influenced by American styling. The large European companies such as Renault, Peugeot, Fiat also developed new post-war designs.

Daimler-Benz returned to production with its modest pre-war Mercedes-Benz 170 model with gasoline or diesel power. By 1951 the company was able to launch its all-new 220 and 300 series, which formed the basis for Daimler-Benz's post-war recovery.

When Mercedes decided to return to competition, in which it had been almost unbeatable during the 1930s, it used components from its 300 series cars as a base. It developed the aerodynamic 300SL (super light) coupe, which proved to be a formidable competitor, winning, among

produce his own car after the war. Influenced by the Packard V-12 engine, he determined that his cars would have V-12s. He had his engineer design a jewel-like, aluminum alloy 1.5 litre 12, later enlarged to 2.0 litres and beyond. His first few cars were rather chunky in appearance, and were mostly intended for competition.

Then in 1949 he introduced the new Type 166 (based on the cc displacement of one cylinder) sports/racing model. It was beautiful as well as fast, and it launched the Ferrari mystique. Ferrari won LeMans in 1949, and would go on to success in building both successful racers and road cars that were exotic as well as expensive. By 1970 Ferrari would be under the control of Italy's giant Fiat.

By the late 1940s and early '50s European manufacturers were introducing their new post-war models. Austin launched it A40 sedan for 1948, and it sold very well. Morris brought out its successful Morris Minor, Rootes its new Hillman

1950 Austin A40, enjoyed brief popularity in North America

1956 Mercedes-Benz 300SL roadster, stunning styling, superb engineering

others, the 1952 LeMans race and the 1952 Carrera Panamericana (Mexican Road Race). Mercedes had intended the 300SL as a competition car only, an interim step on the way to a full return to Grand Prix racing, which it did in 1954 and '55, winning the championship in both years.

Plans changed for the 300SL, however, when Max Hoffman, Daimler-Benz's American distributor based in New York, urged them to make the 300SL a production model. He backed up his conviction with an order for 1000 cars, although he didn't ask Diamler-Benz to change the name. It was reminiscent of the Emil Jellinek order of 1901 that had launched the Mercedes name. Again, Daimler-Benz couldn't afford to refuse, and the production 300SL coupe made its debut in New York in 1954, signalling the increasing importance that Daimler-Benz was placing on the North American market. Hoffman also convinced them to produce the tamer 190SL model, which proved to be another sales success.

The Mercedes-Benz 300SL was a benchmark car that embodied a strong competition record, outstanding engineering, and styling that was not only beautiful but was aerodynamically efficient. Its multi-tube space frame reached half-way up the side of the car, precluding the use of normal doors. The solution was to cut the doors into the roof, resulting in the "Gullwing" nickname that was immediately applied to the coupe. Thus, what had been an engineering necessity quickly became a styling coup, one that would be followed later by others such as DeLorean and Bricklin. The 300 SL also came as a roadster model.

Under the aerodynamic skin was another pioneering achievement: the world's first application of fuel injection to a four-stroke production gasoline engine. Its 300 sedan-derived overhead cam six cylinder engine was tilted 50 degrees to the left to allow a low hood line.

The 1950s was a decade of contradictions. It would be a period of both expansion and contraction: an expansion of production and exports, yet a contraction in the number of automobile companies. With the return of real competition to the industry, old names would merge and/or disappear. Austin and Nuffield (Morris, MG, *et al*) joined in 1952 to become British Motor Corp. Jowett could not save itself with its stylish Lincoln Zephyr-inspired sedan and smart little Jupiter roadster, and the Jowett name disappeared in 1954.

Singer, which had developed its all-new Americanized post-war SM 1500 sedan somewhat resembling the first Kaiser Frazer, as well as a sporty roadster in the MG idiom, became part of the Rootes Group in 1956.

North America, the world's greatest car market, was an irresistible lure for Europe's car makers. Britain, for example, with its "Export or Die" policy after the war, allocated its scarce steel supply among those companies that were exporting their products in return for strong dollars. Thus such British cars as Jaguars and MGs that were igniting the North American interest in sports cars, were almost unobtainable in the home market. Of the cars that Britain exported to North America, sports cars would gradually predominate when their small sedans would prove largely unsuitable for North American driving.

The huge New World market lured many lesser known European manufacturers. Names like Lloyd, Wartburg, Goggomobil, Goliath, Panhard, Moretti, Deutsch-Bonnet, and NSU would appear for a while, then disappear. France, Italy, Germany, Britain, Sweden and others would establish North American beachheads. Almost without exception they would grant franchise rights to North American distributors, and those manufacturers that gained strength eventually established their own North American branch companies.

British Motor Corp.'s first 1959 Austin Mini, front-wheel drive, unbelievable space efficiency

The British Motor Corp.'s tiny Mini, badged as both Austin and Morris, arrived in 1959, and set a new trend in modern automobile layouts. Like the earlier DKW Front, it had its engine mounted laterally in the front, driving the front wheels. Using this compact powertrain configuration, and pushing the small wheels out to the corners of the car, provided space for four passengers and their luggage within an overall length of just 3048 mm (10 feet). It was the work of a brilliant but quirky Turkish-born engineer named Alec Issigonis, who also had the design of the successful post-WWII Morris Minor to his credit.

With the Mini, Issigonis began to lead small car designers away from the rear engine garden path that Porsche and Ledwinka had led many of them down in the 1920s and '30s. It was a master stroke, and BMC would follow it up in the 1960s with larger, very space efficient versions such as the Austin America and Austin 1800.

Unfortunately for BMC, and ultimately for the British car industry, they would squander the early technical lead that Issigonis had given them, and leave the popularization of the cross-engine, front-drive layout to others like the Honda Civic and Volkswagen Golf (initially badged as the Rabbit in North America). The cross-engine, front-drive layout would eventually become the predominant automobile configuration.

While Britain would lose control of its volume car manufacturing industry, it would, ironically, excel in another area: building race cars. Many small English specialty companies, *a la* Colin Chapman and his Lotus enterprise, began producing all types of racers. England became the place in the world to go, whether one was seeking an Indianapolis or LeMans competitor, or a Formula One winner. Engines, however, were usually produced by major automobile manufacturers.

In the late 1950s and into the '60s the German Volkswagen Beetle gradually emerged as the world's leading small car. It would dominate the sixties, and herald Germany's rise to power as a global automobile power.

Also in the late 1950s Japan would begin to venture forth into the export market. Datsun and Toyota began testing the U.S. market in California with their little Datsun Bluebirds and Toyota Toyopets. They would prove to be largely unsuitable for North America, but unlike some other countries, the Japanese persisted in adapting their cars for export markets. They tested and improved, and returned to test again until they made their cars competitive. By the 1970s they were challenging the Volkswagen for small car supremacy.

Besides long-established Datsun and Toyota, there was a newcomer from Japan. Soichiro Honda had started fitting war surplus engines to bicycles right after World War II. This led to the establishment of his motorcycle factory, and ultimately to Honda becoming the world's largest motorcycle manufacturer.

Honda then decided to go into automobiles, and made his first car, a tiny roadster, in 1962. Next came small sedans, which evolved into the 1973 Civic which would launch Honda onto the world's automobile stage. It was followed by the larger Accord, and Honda soon joined Datsun (now Nissan) and Toyota as Japan's Big Three.

As a younger company that was not so bound to the Japanese establishment, Honda was more outward looking, a more international company. It was, for example, the first Japanese automaker to begin mass-producing cars in North America when its Marysville, Ohio plant began turning out Accords in 1982. Every major Japanese

1975 Honda Civic, signalling Japan's rise

manufacturer would follow Honda in establishing plants in North America.

Patterns were beginning to emerge. Unlike North America where the automobile industry had evolved into a monopoly dominated by the Big Three, GM, Ford and Chrysler, the market in Europe, and later in Japan, was keenly competitive. Thus, while automotive technology stagnated in the fat and isolated American industry, it forged ahead in Europe. Such developments as radial tires, disc brakes, fuel injection, rack-and-pinion steering, front-wheel drive, and overhead camshaft, high efficiency engines became the norm in Europe.

While all of this was happening from the 1950s to the '70s, the North American manufac-

turers were producing predominately large, usually V-8 powered, rear-wheel drive gas guzzlers. Thus, when the energy crisis of 1973 arrived, American manufacturers were ill prepared to produce the number of high quality, fuel efficient cars the market suddenly demanded. It was an invitation to Japan to fill a void, and a particularly lucky break for Honda which had just announced its economical little Civic.

The Japanese were quick to adapt the best engineering available, and soon made their cars as competitive as those of the Europeans. This emulation turned into innovation, not only in vehicle engineering, but in mass production methodology. The Japanese developed a major manufacturing advantage called lean production, a significant refinement of the assembly line method of building cars that Henry Ford had inaugurated in 1913.

Pioneered by Toyota in the 1950s and '60s, with the help of American statistical quality control expert Edwards Demming, who was a voice in the wilderness in his home country, lean production reviewed and improved every facet of the mass production system. From a reduction of parts on hand, called just-in-time inventory control, to the time-and-motion study of assemblers, Toyota improved the production efficiency of its factories. It was able to reduce the number of worker hours going into each vehicle to, in some cases, half of European and American levels. And they were able to do this while achieving higher assembly quality. It was a formidable advantage, and a system under which Japan would introduce a new level of efficiency and quality to the total industry. Japan raised the quality bar for automakers the world over, and to remain competitive the global industry would be forced to adapt.

The 1970s would be a pivotal decade for the European and Asian auto industries. Britain would gradually fall into decline due to a failure to keep its cars abreast of the competition in engineering and quality, driven in part by nationalization of some of its car industry, and the heavy hand of militant labour.

A major consolidation occurred in 1968 when British Motor Corp. and Leyland joined to become British Leyland Motor Corp. They later became the Rover Group, and would ultimately end up being owned by Germany's BMW. Most of the British auto industry, including the vaunted Rolls-Royce, eventually came under the control of foreigners. It was a sad decline for an industry that had once been second in production only to the United States.

During the 1970s and '80s many European manufacturers, due to unsuitable cars and/or indifferent service, would withdraw from the world's biggest market, North America. Companies like Peugeot, Fiat and Citroen, while successful at home, were either unwilling or unable to adapt to North American requirements. Those that did, like

1966 Renault Dauphine, beautiful French princess

Mercedes-Benz, BMW, Volkswagen, Saab and Volvo, stayed and prospered.

Renault, after being successful in exporting its utilitarian rear engine 4CV and its lovely little Dauphine in the 1950s and '60s, would gradually decline. It would attempt a comeback by purchasing control of American Motors Corp. in 1980. Its French designed, and American manufactured Alliances and Encores were reasonably successful for a while, but sales ultimately flagged. Its second foray into the North American market had failed, and Renault sold AMC to Chrysler in 1987. With the 1999 takeover of Nissan by Renault, it may again return to the North American market for the third time, perhaps with "badge-engineered" Nissans.

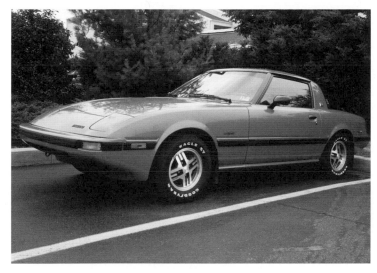

1981 Mazda RX-7, vindicated rotary power

The Japanese industry, on the other hand, grew stronger and more mature in the 1970s. With cars like the Honda Civic and Accord, Datsun 510, Toyota Corolla and Mazda GLC, the Japanese were making durable, good quality family cars that more and more people wanted to buy. And on the sports car scene, while the English who had virtually "owned" the market in the 1950s and '60s, allowed their designs to stagnate, the Japanese took over with such groundbreaking cars as the Datsun 240Z and the Mazda RX-7.

The Mazda RX-7 was an example of Japanese persistence. It was powered by a Wankel rotary combustion engine, a design that had been patented by German engineer Felix Wankel in 1958. The rotary was heralded as a major competitor for the traditional piston engine, and the NSU company of Germany introduced the first rotary powered car, the NSU Sport Prinz, in 1963.

Many companies, including General Motors, American Motors, Curtiss-Wright and Mazda, purchased licences to develop and produce the rotary engine. But it required so much engineering and development work, particularly in the area of rotor sealing, that one by one all but Mazda gave up on it.

Under the dogged direction of Mazda's director of research, Kenichi Yamamoto, the rotary was gradually developed into a durable and practical engine. Mazda would build many rotary powered models, but the one that would make its greatest mark was the RX-7 sports car. The Mazda rotary would really come of age when a four-rotor RX-7 won the LeMans 24-hour race in 1991.

Another development of the 1970s was the beginning of the Korean automobile industry. Korea's giant Hyundai industrial company began assembling British Fords under licence in 1974, and by the 1980s was able, with technical help from Japan's Mitsubishi, to produce its very successful Pony. Although a rather dated, rear-wheel drive design, its low price enabled it to become Canada's best selling small car for a period in the 1980s. Hyundai gradually developed its own technology, and with cars like the Sonata, is now a keen Asian competitor in the world market.

1988 Acura Legend, Japan's march to luxury begins

The Soviet Union had not developed a strong automobile industry. At the luxury end of the market, its efforts were begun in the 1950s with cars called the Zim and the Zil, which used cast-off American designs, principally Packard and General Motors. Production was limited, and the cars were used mostly by government officials.

In the popular price range the Soviets built cars like the Volga and the Moskvitch. The Moskvitch, a model based on a pre-World War II Opel, was launched in 1947. It was a sturdy car, and it was developed over the years to the point that the U.S.S.R. tried exporting it in the late 1960s, but without much success.

The most popular Soviet export model was the Lada, a car based on the Fiat 124 sedan. Assembly began in the late 1960s in a huge plant in the City of Togliatti on the Volga River. A four-wheel drive model called the Niva was also produced, and Ladas were exported to many countries, including Canada, but not, presumably for political reasons, to the United States. Under its totalitarian system U.S.S.R. technology lagged behind the cars of Europe, Asia and North America, The Lada's main attraction was its low price, and exports would never reach significant levels. Lada was still offering cars for sale in Canada in the 1990s.

By the 1980s German cars, particularly Mercedes-Benzes, were considered the most prestigious in the world. While the luxurious Rolls-Royce may still be nominally the best car in the world, the truth was that Rolls-Royce's engineering resources were no match for such companies as Daimler-Benz, General Motors, Ford, BMW, Volkswagen and Toyota. Thus, while Rolls-Royce had the traditional English allure of burled wood and Connolly leather, by the 1990s a BMW V-12 could be found under its hood.

Toward the end of the 1980s the Japanese made their move into the top level of prestige cars. It started with the 1987 Legend from Honda's Acura division, which was followed three years later by the Lexus from Toyota, and the Infiniti from Nissan (formerly Datsun). Lexus and Infiniti would produce ultra-luxury cars that independent studies proclaimed were the equal of the Mercedes-Benzes and BMWs from Germany. And they scored higher in customer surveys than the vaunted American Cadillac, which for many years had called itself "The Standard of the World."

While all of this activity was taking place in free Europe and Asia, automobile technology was virtually dormant behind the Iron Curtain. The rather primitive engineering of East European cars was vividly demonstrated with the fall of the Berlin wall fell in 1989, which brought a stream of little Trabants smoking across the border from the German Democratic Republic (East Germany). Their technology was based on pre-WWII DKW engineering, and the heavy hand of Communism had retarded their modernization for over 40 years.

With the market opened up, Eastern manufacturers would soon come under the influence of Western methods. Volkswagen, for example, purchased Czechoslovakia's Skoda in 1991, and was soon producing a state-of-the-art Skoda.

As the century was coming to an end, the mergers, acquisitions and take-overs that had long been a hallmark of the industry continued. What had happened in America earlier, began to

1969 Trabant, personifying stifled competition

speed up in Europe and Japan. Ford bought Britain's Jaguar in 1989, owned Aston Martin, held a major share in Japan's Mazda, and then bought Sweden's Volvo Car Co. Volkswagen purchased Rolls-Royce, although ironically, BMW was able to buy the name. BMW also owned Britain's Rover Group, and General Motors had a half interest in Saab and owned part of Japan's Suzuki. Then in the biggest merger of all, Daimler Benz and Chrysler joined in 1998 to become DaimlerChrysler. In 1999 Renault took a controlling interest in debt-laden Nissan.

With this sudden rash of consolidation activity, driven by intense competition and worldwide production over-capacity, it began to appear that the prediction of the world's automobile manufacturing being controlled by 10 or 12 giants by the turn of the century could come true.

From its cradle in Germany, to its mass production in America, to its lean production in Japan, the automobile has travelled a long way since 1885. The automotive world was truly becoming a smaller place.

A Diverse Collection
of
Cars and Companies

AMERICAN AUSTIN/BANTAM CAR COMPANY

If ever there was a propitious time for an economy car to arrive on the scene it should have been 1930. With the Depression starting to suck the life out of the economy, a car that went 40 miles on a gallon of gasoline sounded like exactly what the North American market required. It was at the other end of the automotive spectrum from the 16 cylinder Cadillacs and Marmons that had been conceived in the flamboyant twenties, but were now hopelessly out of step with the times.

This new car was the diminutive American Austin, an Americanized version of the English Austin Seven that Herbert Austin had conceived in 1921, and the Austin Motor Co. had put on the market the following year. It was a kind of English equivalent of Henry Ford's Model T, an everyman's car that was barely larger than the motorcycle-and-sidecar combination it was meant to replace. It proved so popular that it inspired a French version, the Rosengart, and a German one, the Dixi, built under licence by BMW.

Encouraged by the success of his Seven during the 1920s, both at home and abroad, Herbert Austin decided to take his tiny car to the world's largest automobile market, North America. Armed with four Austin Sevens, he set sail for New York in 1929. His goal was to make arrangements to manufacture and sell his cars in the United States.

A deal was consummated with some American businessmen, the American Austin Car Co. was incorporated in Delaware, and a factory was acquired in Butler, Pennsylvania. An office was set up in Detroit where engineers went to work adapting the Austin to the American market.

The most obvious need was to convert from right-to left-hand drive. The styling was considered a little lacklustre for the New World, so former Russian Count and famed stylist Alexis de Sakhnoffsky of Austin's body supplier, Hayes Body Co., dressed up the little English pram with some two-tone paint and disc wheels. The engine was also enlarged slightly from 42.5 cubic inches (697 cc) to 45.6 (747 cc), and horsepower increased from 10 to 13.

Following the stock market crash in October 1929, circumstances had dramatically changed when Herbert Austin returned to Butler in January

1931 American Austin sedan, popular in Britain, failed in America

1930 to announce the start of production. It was a change that should have augured well for an economy car.

Three American Austins were displayed at New York and Chicago trade shows. Some 4000 dealers signed up to sell this new small car, and when orders reportedly exceeded 50,000, Herbert Austin returned to England full of optimism, and visions of a seven dollar royalty on each car.

An unexpected start-up delay was caused by a skirmish with Grand Rapids, Michigan, which was trying to entice American Austin to move the operation to their city. As the home of the Austin Automobile Co. from 1901 to 1921, an American firm totally unrelated to the English

Austin operation, they felt they had a spiritual, if not a legal right to build this new Austin.

Grand Rapids was also the home of Austin's body builder, the Hayes Body Co. After local Butler citizens rallied behind American Austin, and raised close to a half million dollars to support it, the company remained in Butler. Cars finally began rolling off the assembly line at American Austin in May 1930.

When the cars reached showrooms a month later they attracted thousands of visitors. Here was something totally different. Although it bore a passing similarity to a contemporary Chevrolet, it was like an optical illusion. Its fenders, headlamps and radiator shell resembled the American car, and its horizontal beltline and hood louvres imparted an impression of length, but it was hard to believe that the American Austin was really that small.

The Austin was more than two feet (610 mm) shorter and 16 inches (406 mm) narrower than any other American car. Its wheelbase was a tiny 75 inches (1905 mm), and the tread a narrow 40 inches (1016 mm). Overall length was 122 inches (3099 mm), and it weighed just 1130 pounds (513 kg). It came in three models, a coupe, roadster and delivery van. The cars could accommodate two passengers and carry a small amount of cargo behind the seat.

The tiny side-valve four cylinder engine looked little bigger than the battery, which also resided under the hood, a novel location in an America car. Apart from its size the tiny power-plant was normal in appearance, with the exception of the generator which was mounted at right angles to the engine and driven by a gear on the camshaft.

In spite of the initial dealer response, and the widespread public attention, American Austin sales were disappointing. As it turned out, the public's reaction was more curiosity than genuine interest. The car never seemed to dispel the notion that it was a kind of off-beat novelty, and even though the Austin got 40 miles-per-gallon, its most outstanding feature, only 8558 people actually bought one in 1930. The fact that it was priced about the same as a Model A Ford roadster was no doubt an important factor.

The company broadened the lineup for 1931 with the addition of two new coupe models and a cabriolet, but discontinued the van. It didn't help, however, because the year-end reckoning indicated that less than 1400 cars had been sold.

The plant went into 1932 operating only intermittently, and when 1500 partially completed cars piled up on the assembly line, bankruptcy seemed imminent. This would undoubtedly have been the end of American Austin had it not been for the intervention of a dynamic Atlanta entrepreneur named Ray Evans. Evans operated a successful string of Florida car dealerships, and was the Austin's top salesman. He bought the unsold inventory of cars, had them completed, and sold them through his dealerships at cut-rate prices.

Evans's program was so successful that he was asked to take responsibility for reviving the plant. He agreed, and under his aegis American Austin turned out 3846 cars in 1932. He was able to keep the plant producing through 1933, and to increase output to almost 5000 cars. By 1934, however, even Evans's magic could no longer sustain the enterprise and Austin production trickled to a stop.

Except for a skeleton staff engaged in filling parts orders, and doing a little custom machine shop work, the Butler plant was deserted during 1935 and '36. It seemed to be simply marking time until disposal of the stock and equipment could take place.

But the ebullient Mr. Evans was nothing if not persistent, and had never lost his Austin enthusiasm. He still believed there was a North American market for an economical small car, and was able to convince Austin's creditors that he could rejuvenate the carbuilder. With little option other than scrapping the plant, they agreed to sell Evans the operation for a paltry $5000, which was below scrap value.

The company was reorganized in 1936 as the American Bantam Car Co., and de Sakhnoffsky was again called in to update the styling of the little car, for which he charged a mere $300 fee.

Engineering improvements such as full pressure lubrication, a higher compression ratio and a synchromesh transmission were made.

The new 1938 Bantam was introduced in September 1937, and exhibiting the hope that springs eternal, 3000 dealers signed on. Alas, amid plans for 10,000 cars for 1938, less than 3000 were produced. In spite of the addition of a woody wagon for 1939, and more mechanical improvements for 1940, sales slipped to less than 1000 in '39 and 800 in '40.

Although it should have been right in tune with the hard economic times, it was

1938 American Bantam roadster, lilliputian beauty

obvious that the Bantam could not survive. Before it was written off completely, however, there was one postscript that enshrined American Bantam's name forever in the annals of automotive history: it designed and built the very first Jeep.

In 1940 the U.S. Army issued tenders to 135 automotive and related companies inviting them to submit prototypes of a 1/4-ton, 4-wheel-drive utility vehicle in just 49 days. American Bantam was the only company that met this arduous deadline. Its little "Bantam Recon Car," was found acceptable, but Bantam's production capacity was woefully inadequate to meet the military's requirement. To American Bantam's bitter disappointment, the army had no choice but to turn to the Willys-Overland version. Although American Bantam did get to build 1500 of them, and many Jeep trailers, the big Jeep contract went to Willys, with Ford also building many of them under licence.

American Motors Corporation

The purchase of American Motors Corporation by Chrysler in 1987 marked the end of an epic struggle that had been the hallmark of the North American automobile industry from its beginning. The disappearance of AMC was the final chapter in the inexorable march to oligopoly that gradually eliminated one after another of the non-Big Three (GM, Ford and Chrysler) automakers.

This industrial Darwinism had even brought Chrysler to the brink of extinction in the early 1980s. It was pulled back by the charismatic leadership of Lee Iacocca, who thereby earned a place in the history books beside such company saviours as Alfred P. Sloan, Jr., Walter Chrysler and Henry Ford II. But before the end of the century, the Big Three would be the Big Two as Chrysler amalgamated with Germany's Daimler Benz in 1998 to become DaimlerChrysler.

In the beginning hundreds of enterprising blacksmiths, bicycle manufacturers and carriage makers entered and quickly left the burgeoning automobile business. One of the survivors, Henry Ford I, would thrive, but only after three attempts. His sturdy, affordable Model Ts rolled off the world's first auto assembly line fast enough to make Ford the world's dominant automobile company.

General Motors under Sloan's management, and Chrysler, formed by Walter Chrysler out of the Maxwell Motor Corporation in 1925, gradually rose to challenge Ford. This battle of the titans would lead to the demise of all the rest.

Two of the oldest and most respected automobile names, Nash and Hudson, would, as American Motors Corporation, last the longest of the independents. Their merger to form AMC in 1954 brought roots that extended back even further than Ford or General Motors.

Nash was the older, dating from the Thos. B. Jeffery Co. of Kenosha, Wisconsin, a bicycle maker that began building cars in 1902. Their first one was called the Rambler, after one of their bicycles. Jeffery became the Nash Motor Co. in 1917 when Charles Nash bought it after leaving the presidency of General Motors.

Over the years Nash built a reputation for sound reliable cars. The company was progressive, bringing to market such features as unitized construction, "Weather Eye" air conditioning, and seats that converted into a bed. It merged with appliance maker Kelvinator to become Nash-Kelvinator in 1937.

In spite of production that fell below 15,000 in 1933, Nash survived the Depression. Its World War II products included aircraft engines and cargo trailers, and after the war it resumed building vehicles of pre-war design. Its new Airflyte model of 1949 was well received with its enclosed wheels, unit construction and one-piece windshield.

In 1950 Nash surprised the world with its compact Rambler, reviving an old Nash name. Riding on a 100-inch (2540 mm) wheelbase and looking like a smaller version of its larger Airflyte siblings, it was a sensation. Its pre-war Nash 600 components provided adequate performance and excellent fuel economy. According to Tom McCahill, *Mechanix Illustrated* magazine's pioneering car tester, it was "as cute as a cupcake."

During this period Nash also engaged in a couple of Anglo-American ventures. The first was the attractive Nash-Healey, one of the earliest post-war production sports cars; Crosley of Cincinnati, Ohio, was the first with its Hotshot. The Nash-Healey beat the Chevrolet Corvette to market by two years.

The chassis was supplied by the Donald Healey Co. of England, and power came from a big Nash Ambassador six. It was fast, durable and

1904 Rambler, a long surviving name

handsome. One finished third in the famous LeMans, France 24-hour endurance race in 1952, beaten only by two of the invincible new Mercedes-Benz 300SLs.

The other Nash hybrid was the Nash Metropolitan, a tiny American-designed runabout that looked like a caricature of the big Airflytes. It had an English Austin four cylinder engine, and was built from 1954 to 1962.

Hudson could also trace its roots back a long way, although not quite as far as Nash. It was started in 1909 when four ex-Oldsmobile employees, including Roy D. Chapin who later became general manager of American Motors,

1931 Hudson Speedster, elegance and performance

1956 Nash Rambler, American Motors' saviour

formed a car company. Detroit department store magnate Joseph L. Hudson provided start-up funds of $90,000, so the car was named after him. Production began in the defunct Aerocar plant in Detroit in July 1909. By July 1910 they had built over 4000 cars, a first year industry record.

Hudson specialized in sturdy, reliable cars, and prospered over the years to the extent that by 1929, the eve of the Depression, it had produced 300,000 cars. It spun off other nameplates such as Essex, which popularized the affordable four-door sedan, and Terraplane, known for its excellent performance.

By using relatively large, powerful engines Hudson built a well deserved reputation for high performance. During the 1930s it held almost every American Automobile Association speed record, many by the famous English driver John Cobb.

After WWII work that included aircraft and munitions, Hudson also returned to pre-war cars. Then in 1948 it stunned the world with its dramatic "Step Down Design," accomplished by using a dropped floor pan in its unit construction body. The Hudson was low, wide and stable, which combined with its big 5.0 litre six cylinder engine, enabled the Hudson Hornet to dominate National Association for Stock Car Auto Racing for several years.

Alas "Win on Sunday, Sell on Monday" didn't work for Hudson, and sales gradually fell from 131,915 in 1951 to 66,143 in 1953. A venture into the compact field with its Jet model lasted only a couple of years. Hudson and Nash needed

1965 AMC Rambler Marlin, AMC's fastback attempt

1971 AMC Gremlin, leading the sub-compacts

partners; the stage was set for the amalgamation in 1954 that formed American Motors.

AMC sold cars with both Nash and Hudson nameplates, although they really were Nashes. Then in 1957 the Nash and Hudson names were discontinued; from 1958 to 1970 all AMC cars, with a few exceptions such as the Javelin, would be Ramblers.

During the 1960s AMC attempted to go head to head with the Big Three in all classes: the compact Rambler; the Rambler Classic, later the Rebel, and even later the Matador; and the luxury Ambassador. AMC's George Romney, who later became Governor of Michigan, sold the sensibly sized Ramblers by railing against the Big Three's "gas guzzling dinosaurs." He pulled Rambler up to third place in sales by 1961.

AMC joined the fastback crowd in 1965 with the Marlin. Based first on the Rambler Classic,

and then on the Ambassador, it disappeared in 1967. This was followed in 1968 by the Javelin, AMC's entry in the pony-car market. A shortened version of the Javelin called the AMX appeared mid-year.

In 1970 the Rambler American metamorphosed into the Hornet, a comedown for that grand old Hudson name. In mid-year AMC beat the Big Three into the subcompact segment when its imaginative and talented styling chief, Richard Teague, the master of the low-cost makeover, chopped the rear end off the Hornet to produce the Gremlin. Then in one of its shrewdest moves, AMC purchased the Kaiser-Jeep Corporation, thereby acquiring the Jeep, one of the world's most famous automotive nameplates.

AMC had a strong Canadian connection. Hudsons were assembled in Tilbury, Ontario,

1977 AMC Pacer station wagon, the "Glass Turtle"

1986 AMC Eagle station wagon, four-wheel drive traction, car-like comfort

before and after WWII, and Nashes were built in Toronto in the early '50s. AMC established a new assembly plant in Brampton, Ontario, in 1961 which produced both cars and Jeeps. In the mid-80s, now under Renault's control, it constructed an ultra-modern facility in Bramalea, Ontario.

American Motors struggled through the '70s, stretching Teague's talents to make old cars look new. Its only all new design was the "glass turtle" Pacer, the big small car that came out in 1975. Originally designed for a rotary engine, it got AMC's inline six squeezed under the hood, which encroached on interior room. The Pacer was heavy, not particularly economical, and had mediocre performance. It was discontinued in 1980.

One pioneering contribution AMC made in North America was the four-wheel drive pas-senger car. This was the AMC Eagle introduced in 1980, and based on the Concord (formerly Hornet). It appealed to the motorist who wanted all-wheel traction but didn't want a utility-type vehicle like the Jeep.

AMC would come under the control of Renault in the '80s and together they built and marketed French designed cars in North America. French cars have not enjoyed lasting popularity over here, and this time was no exception. Cars like the Alliance and Encore had brief acceptance, but quickly faded from favour. Renault finally gave up on North American and sold AMC to the Chrysler Corporation in 1987, which turned it into its Jeep-Eagle Division. With this acquisition the last chapter of the independents' struggle for survival was written.

90

Auburn Automobile Company

Although the Auburn car could trace its ancestry back to the turn of the century, it took a high-flying entrepreneur named Errett Lobban Cord to extend its popularity beyond its namesake town in northeastern Indiana. Under Cord's ownership, Auburn went from near bankruptcy to one of the brightest stars on the automotive scene, and then quickly disappeared.

In 1900 brothers Frank and Morris Eckhart, owners of the Eckhart Carriage Co. in Auburn, Indiana, got interested in motor vehicles. After building and selling a few hand-built cars, they formed the Auburn Automobile Co. By 1903 they had built their first production car, a one-cylinder, chain drive machine which they exhibited at the Chicago Auto Show.

Orders came in, and by 1905 a 2-cylinder engine was added. A four cylinder came in 1909 (the twin was dropped in 1911), and a six in 1912. Auburn enjoyed modest success using components such as frames, steering gears, axles and engines largely obtained from outside suppliers.

Auburn remained largely a regional enterprise, and by the late teens the company began languishing financially. It was rescued in 1919 by a consortium of Chicago businessmen who bought control from the Eckharts. The best known of these was chewing gum magnate William Wrigley, Jr. Unfortunately they didn't know much about the car business.

With new management and financial stability, Auburn set out to expand its horizons. It brought out a car called the Beauty-Six, which unfortunately arrived during the post-World War I recession. When better times arrived the neophyte owners were unable to capitalize on them. Sales declined until by 1924 production was down to about six cars per day, and there was an inventory of several hundred unsold Auburns.

The stage was set for the arrival of E.L. Cord. As a top flight salesman of Moon cars in Chicago, the 30 year old Cord had galloping enthusiasm and a five-figure income. He was seen by Auburn's management as just the kind of man they needed to rescue their faltering company.

Cord struck a deal, which, if Auburn prospered, allowed him to gain control of the company. He arrived as general manager of Auburn in

1924. In addition to those unsold 700 Auburns, he met a dispirited staff and bleak prospects.

But Cord was undaunted. He realised that he had to sell the sizzle as well as the steak, that the automobile business was as much, or more, about style as it was about engineering.

Cord set out to unload the unsold Auburns. He had the workers lower the cars by cutting three inches out of the top bows. He then had the cars repainted in bright appealing colours, which he accented with nickel plated trim. Within a short time the entire inventory of Auburns was sold, bringing badly needed profit to the company.

Cord then turned his attention to new Auburn models. Although not an engineer, he realized that engines with more cylinders meant more prestige. For the 1925 model lineup he badgered the company's engineers into squeezing a Lycoming straight eight engine into a six cylinder body. The cars were also freshened up in appearance with two-tone paint and a beltline that curved up over the cowl and swept forward on top of the hood to form a vee at the radiator cap. It was a styling motif that would mark Auburns for many years.

With new styling and an eight cylinder engine, Auburn sales took off. Not surprisingly it had vaulted Cord into the position of president of Auburn by 1926. This was also the year of Auburn's last four cylinder car, and sales rose to over 7,000. They reached almost 10,000 in '27,

and about 12,000 in '28 when the dashing new boat-tailed speedster model was introduced.

With an eye to publicity, Cord sent Auburns in pursuit of speed records. An Auburn set a record of 108.46 mph on the sands of Daytona Beach, averaged 84.7 mph for 24 hours at Atlantic City, and won the hill climb trophy at Pikes Peak, Colorado.

Once secure in the presidency, Cord went on a buying spree. He acquired the Indianapolis-based Duesenberg Motor Co., engine supplier Lycoming Manufacturing, McFarlan Motor Car Co., and Columbia Axle. He would later add Stinson Aircraft, Checker Cab, New York Shipbuilding, and Century Airlines. He brought his acquisitions together under a holding company, the Cord Corp., in 1929.

Because the mighty model J Duesenberg, which Cord had asked the Duesenberg brothers, Fred and August to design, and the newly introduced 1929 L-29 front-wheel drive Cord were large, prestige models with a limited market, Cord knew that a more popular priced Auburn was needed. With flashy new models introduced for 1929, and the record-setting publicity, yearly Auburn sales shot up to about 18,000.

The onset of the Depression caused by the stock market collapse late in 1929 slowed Auburn's 1930 registrations. Surprisingly, they rebounded to over 29,000 in 1931, which would prove to be its highest year ever. Almost in defiance of the Depression, Auburn dropped its six cylinder engine and small eights in favour of large, luxury, 98-hp eight cylinder models.

In even greater defiance, Cord introduced the Auburn Twelve for 1932, powered by a 160 hp, 6.4 litre (391 cu in.) Lycoming V-12 engine. At prices of under $1000, 8-and 12-cylinder Auburns represented the most car for the money in the world.

But the Depression was a formidable foe. Auburn sales declined to 11,646 for 1932, and then to just over 5,000 for the carryover 1933 models.

In an attempt to revive 1934 sales Auburn brought back a price-leading six cylinder engine. The V-12 was quietly phased out. New aerodynamic styling also came for 1934 in an attempt to boost sales, which it did for the last part of the year, pushing them to over 5,500.

But it was recognized that extraordinary measures were required for survival. Cord turned over control of the recovery attempt to Duesenberg's president Harold Ames, who engaged the assistance of Duesenberg's stylist Gordon Buehrig and chief engineer August Duesenberg.

Ames, Buehrig and Duesenberg set to work for 1935. As an image builder they revived the boat-tailed speedster model after a year's absence, and gave it new front end styling. But the more significant change was under the hood.

Working with the Schwitzer-Cummins Co. of Indianapolis, August Duesenberg developed a

1932 Auburn Phaeton, 1930s elegance

centrifugal supercharger for the straight-eight engine. This boosted horsepower from 115 to 150. To let the world know that it was supercharged, Buehrig had four flexible chrome plated exhaust pipes curving out of the left side of the hood.

The 1935 supercharged Auburn boat-tailed speedster was a sensation. E.L. Cord sent one to the Bonneville salt flats where racer Ab Jenkins drove it to 70 new speed records, including 500 miles at 103 mph.

Cord had each production speedster fitted with a dashboard plaque certifying that it had been driven at a specific speed, always in excess of 100 mph, by Ab Jenkins or another racer. But in keeping with Cord's occasionally opportunistic approach to business, this may not have been the complete truth. Former Auburn employees have

1935 Auburn Boattail Speedster, speed and panache

alleged that the plaques were sometimes fitted before assembly was completed!

Despite the revived speedster, and supercharging, Auburn sales continued at about the same level for 1935, and the company carried over its models unchanged into 1936. This was the year that E.L.Cord brought out his second Cord car (the L-29 had been discontinued in 1932), the stunning new Buehrig-designed, front-wheel drive 810 model. Its sensational "coffin nose," low profile styling, hidden headlamps, and lack of running boards, stole the show from the Auburns.

Nineteen-thirty-six would be Auburn's last year, when less than 2,000 were built. E.L. Cord managed to continue Cord production into 1937 before it too succumbed to the ravages of the Depression. It is ironic that Auburn's most revered and collectible model, the supercharged boat-tailed Speedster, was created in the company's dying days.

E.L. Cord sold his automotive interests and moved to other endeavours, including convincing the U.S. Securities and Exchange Commission that he had not used questionable practices to boost the value of his corporate stock. He died in 1974 at the age of 80.

Austin-Healey Sprite

The 1950s were innocent times compared with today's computerized sophistication. In the automotive world, a Chevy meant one kind and size of car, as did Ford and Plymouth. Hardly anybody even knew about air pollution from cars, let alone worried about it, and gasoline was cheap and plentiful.

And safety? The public apparently wasn't interested. In 1956 Ford offered a number of safety features such as a deep dish steering wheel, and padded instrument panels and sun visors, and as the saying around Detroit went, "Ford sold safety and Chevy sold cars."

This is a tale about a car, the Austin-Healey

1959 Austin Healey Sprite, affordable sport

Sprite, that was the essence of 1950s simplicity, but which yielded driving fun way beyond its basic mechanical credentials.

Most of the cars we drove then were pretty prosaic, but a new element had been introduced in the late '40s and early '50s in the form of the English sports car. The MG was the first to reach our shores in any number, and the MG TC and TD roadsters became the quintessential definition of what a sports car was: fun to drive and almost totally impractical. Then Jaguar came along with its fabulous XK120 model, which was followed by the Triumph TR2 and the Austin-Healey 100.

Then, as later, the trend was to gradually make cars larger and more expensive. The Triumph went through several iterations, as did the Austin-Healey, and even the entry-level sports car, the MG. The classic clamshell fenders of the MG TC and TD gave way to the semi-modern TF, and in 1956, to the rather bland envelope body of the MGA. And prices kept going up.

By the mid-50s it was apparent to Leonard Lord, head of the British Motor Corp., the company formed in 1952 by the merger of Britain's two largest automakers, Austin and the Nuffield Organization (Morris, *et al.*), that there was a need to return to basics in the sports car market. The entry-level sports car enthusiast had been abandoned. BMC needed something at the low end of the scale to fill the gap it had created by moving the MG up-market.

Powel Crosley's Hotshot and Super Sports models in America had held out some promise for first-time sports-car buyers, and although somewhat crudely assembled, they had some quite advanced features for their time. These included an oversquare engine, overhead camshaft engine, and disc brakes in 1949. But Crosley's company had failed by 1952.

Lord knew who to see about such a project, his old friend Donald Healey. Healey and his sons ran the Donald Healey Motor Co. of Warwick, England, where they built sports cars, notably the Silverstone model. But they were always available for outside contracts, and seemed to do more business helping other companies realize their sports-car building dreams than they did manufacturing their own cars.

Healey had collaborated with Nash Motors of the U.S. on the Nash-Healey sports car, which had excelled in competition, but unfortunately failed in the showroom due largely to too high a price. And Healey and Lord had worked together in the development of the popular Austin-Healey 100 sports car.

To keep the price down, Healey knew he would have to keep the design of the little sportster simple and basic, and use as many existing components as possible. Fortunately, BMC had plenty to choose from.

The tiny Austin A-35 sedan provided the coil spring front suspension, four-speed transmission and rear axle. Power came from the 948 cc (58 cu in.) BMC A-series overhead valve inline four pioneered by the Austin A30/35, and used in the Morris Minor. It was, of course, in the true British sports car tradition, fitted with twin S.U. carburetors for the Sprite, which helped boost horsepower to 43 from the Minor's 37.

Morris Minor type rack-and-pinion steering was used, and the rear suspension was by basic quarter elliptic leaf springs. These concentrated rear suspension loads near the middle of the car, and the rear end of the vehicle, thus freed from having to support any of the weight, could be quite light. The curb weight was only 662 kg (1459 lb).

The Sprite was named after a Riley sports car of the 1930s (Nuffield had bought Riley in 1938). It had its simple but well proved hardware wrapped in a steel-monocoque (unit construction) envelope body, the first in a British sports car. The lines were rudimentary but attractive, the only jarring note being the headlamps, which were semi-recessed into the hood and stood up like the eyes of a frog. Almost immediately the Sprite was given its "Bugeye" or "Frogeye" nickname.

The original design had called for concealed headlamps that flipped up, but cost considerations eliminated them. As it turned out, the bug-eye headlamps would redound to the Sprite's favour and become its most distinctive styling feature.

Further cost-cutting was evident in the elimination of a trunk lid. This made it awkward to access the spare tire and limited luggage space behind the two bucket seats, but it did contribute to a body that was sturdy and resistant to twisting, a common problem in open cars. Also, the windshield did not fold down as it had in the MG T-series.

Access to the engine, front suspension and steering was excellent because the whole front section of the body, including the hood, fenders and headlamps, hinged upward alligator style, looking for all the world like it was going to "eat" the attendant. Care had to be taken with the somewhat flimsy props or that, in fact, could happen.

The Sprite was really diminutive, riding on a 2032 mm (80 in.) wheelbase, and being only 3480 mm (137 in.) in over-all length. It stood just 1219 mm (48 in.) high with the top up.

The Bug-eye Sprite was built from May, 1958, to April, 1961, by which time almost 50,000 had been produced. They were an instant success, both on the road and the track, because of their reasonable initial price (under $2000), ease of maintenance, excellent yet forgiving handling, and quick precise steering.

Performance, however, according to *Road & Track* magazine (8/58), could only be termed moderate. They recorded a zero to 60 mph (96 km/h) time of 20.8 seconds, and a top speed of 78.5 mph (125 km/h).

When Bugeye production was discontinued in 1961, it was replaced by the Mark II, which had more horizontal lines and headlamps that were conventional, but not nearly so distinctive. It also got a trunk lid, and a regular rear-hinged hood. At this time the A-H Sprite was joined by a "badge engineered" MG version called the Midget, reviving a name from the T-series MGs. These "Spridgets" were identical except for name, trim and grille, the MG version getting the traditional MG vertical bar type.

In addition to its more conventional looks, the Mark II Sprite got a slight increase in power, from 48 to 50, thanks to higher compression, larger carburetors and a few other changes.

Then for 1963 came a welcome increase in displacement to 1098 cc, which brought horsepower up to 55. This reduced the zero to 60 (96) acceleration time from 19.6 to 18.3 seconds, although the top speed of 85 (137) was unchanged (*Road & Track* 8/63). It also got front disc brakes.

In the spring of 1964 the Mark III was announced. The original quarter elliptic springs were replaced by semi-elliptics, and better breathing improved output to 59 horsepower.

The Mark IV (and last) version of the Sprite arrived for 1967. Engine displacement was again increased, to 1275 cc, which brought horsepower up to 65. This improved the zero to 60 (96) time to 14.7 seconds, and top speed to 93 mph (150 km/h). It also got wind-up windows.

The Sprite would continue largely unchanged until it was discontinued in 1970. The MG Midget would be carried on for another 10 years.

Most of the Sprites were exported to North America, but alas, due to the unit construction many have succumbed to rust. While the Sprite was basic and simple, it accomplished its goal of returning to sports car fundamentals. Countless sports car enthusiasts still recall them fondly, especially what many consider to be the "real" Sprite, the 1958 to '61 Bugeye.

Buick Skylark – 1953–1954

Buick has a long and proud history as part of the General Motors family. It was formed as an automobile manufacturer in 1903 by a Detroit plumbing contractor and inventor named David Dunbar Buick, whose major claim to fame had been discovering the way to fix porcelain to iron plumbing fixtures.

In 1904 the company was moved to Flint, Michigan, where it was taken over by Flint carriage magnate Billy Durant who wanted to get into automobile manufacturing. Buick, along with Cadillac, would form the backbone of Durant's General Motors Co. which he established in 1908.

1953 Buick Skylark, fifties elegance

A feature of Buick from the very beginning was its overhead valve engine in which the valves were in the cylinder head above the pistons, rather than beside them in the engine block. It was a trademark that Buick would stay true to during its entire history. David Buick and employees Eugene Richard and Walter Marr cooperated in developing the overhead valve engine for what is probably the first Buick prototype of 1903 (there is some dispute here; Marr built a car in 1901 which may have also been called a Buick).

Overhead valves were patented under Richard's name, and they gave the two-cylinder Buick powerplant better breathing and more compact combustion chambers than the side-valve engine, enabling it to produce more power. Overhead valves were at the heart of Buick's excellent performance, and following the sale of the first production Buick in 1904, other orders soon followed.

On the strength of its efficient little engine the Buick quickly gained a reputation as a reliable, good performing car. This, coupled with Durant's entrepreneurial drive – one of his first moves was to increase company capitalization from $75,000 to $1.5 million – soon made Buick one of the largest automobile manufacturers in America. It was second in sales only to Ford in 1907 and '08, the dawn of Henry Ford's Model T era.

As part of the General Motors conglomerate,

Buick continued to prosper, even though GM was undergoing upheavals in the boardroom. GM was financially over-extended by 1910 and the bankers took control away from Durant that year, but not before he had built up a superb Buick racing team headed by "Wild Bob" Burman and Louis Chevrolet. Buick would win the first-ever race at the new Indianapolis Speedway (not the Indy 500) and garner extensive speed records and publicity.

Buick got a four cylinder engine in 1906, and a six in 1914. Then in 1931 Buick went exclusively to eights, introducing three new straight-eight engines, all with overhead valves of course. Inline eights would remain a Buick hallmark for over 20 years, until its V-8 appeared for 1953.

There was a lot to celebrate, then, when Buick's 50th anniversary rolled around in 1953. It had survived and thrived through five decades in an industry that had seen hundreds of casualties. It had held a consistent fourth place in sales since 1947, behind Chevrolet, Ford and Plymouth, and would do so again in 1953. And it had its new, powerful, short-stroke overhead valve V-8 engine.

What better way to mark its first half century than with a glamorous image car. With the economy now fully recovered from World War II, and the Korean conflict ending, the American automobile industry was in command of all it surveyed. Not only Buick, but its luxury corporate sisters Cadillac and Oldsmobile, were also yearning for some cachet by offering exclusive flagship models. So Buick's luxurious new Skylark would be accompanied in the marketplace by the Cadillac Eldorado and the Oldsmobile Fiesta, all convertibles and all expensive.

Buick based the Skylark on the big Roadmaster platform, which gave it a wheelbase of 3086 mm (121.5 in.). Its overall length was 5273 mm (207.6 in.) and it tipped the scales at a substantial 1961 kg (4316 lb). Buick called the Skylark a sports car, but in truth it was about the furthest thing from real sports cars, like the English MG and Jaguar, or even the new Chevrolet Corvette, as one could imagine.

Power came from Buick's oversquare (bore and stroke of 4.00 by 3.20 in.) 5.3 litre (322 cu in.) Roadmaster V-8 that developed 188 horsepower @ 4000 rpm, and 300 lb-ft of torque @ 2400. Its 8.5:1 compression ratio was said to be the U.S. industry's highest. Power was sent to the rear wheels through Buick's two-speed "Twin Turbine Dynaflow" automatic transmission.

Buick had pioneered the use of the automobile torque converter in American cars in 1948, and it used two turbines in the converter, which it claimed gave a 10 percent torque increase. This was intended to compensate for having only two gear ratios in the transmission.

The new V-8, which had its valves set vertically in the combustion chambers to keep it narrower, hence the name "vertical valve" engine, developed enough power and torque to endow the big Buick with excellent performance. According to estimates based on other Buick models tested (Buick didn't let its Skylark into the hands of writers), it could launch the Skylark from zero to 60 mph (96 km/h) in times as low as 12 seconds – if one started in low and manually shifted the Dynaflow into high. Starting off in Drive could add two or three seconds to the 0-60 (96) time. Top speed was reported to be approximately 105 mph (169 km/h).

But as good as the Skylark's performance was, there was little doubt that is was the beautiful styling that sold every one of the 1690 two-door convertibles that were built. Buick stylists pulled out all the stops. The result was that in addition to being state-of-the-art in American automotive engineering, it was also a styling leader.

Touted as "Buick's answer to the European sports car," it was introduced in June 1952 as a '53 model. The body fenderline was nicely notched just behind the doors. Chromed "sweepspear" trim mouldings started just aft of the headlamps and swept down and back to the rear wheels, and then curved up and over the beautifully rounded wheel opening. Stylists wisely deleted the "ventiports," commonly called port holes, that had graced the front fenders or hoods of every Buick since 1949.

The wheels were also things of beauty. Designed

to Buick specifications by Kelsey-Hayes, the 40-spoke chromed wire wheels set in painted wheel wells were one of the prettiest aspects of the Skylark. Although the Skylark wasn't a sports car, in spite of Buick's claims, those wire wheels would match the beauty of any sports car.

The overall height of the Skylark was brought below five feet (1524 mm) by cutting down the windshield some four inches (102 mm) compared with the Roadmaster. The body was also lowered slightly, and ground clearance was reduced a little.

If the Skylark was a beauty on the outside, it was also luxurious and fully appointed on the inside. It carried a complete complement of standard equipment, as befitted an image car with a price close to $5000, when $5000 was a lot of money. The upholstery was leather and the gauges were set in an engine-turned instrument panel. As the final touch of class, the owner's signature was placed in the lucite steering wheel hub, along with a picture of the first Buick.

In addition to the automatic transmission, it was also equipped with power assisted brakes and steering. The top, windows and seats were actuated by hydraulic cylinders. Even the "Selectronic" radio's antenna was electrically powered. Air conditioning was available for the first time on Buicks in 1953. It's a good thing that Buick changed from a 6-to a 12-volt electrical system that year to handle the load.

The Skylark was intended to be a one-year model to mark Buick's golden anniversary, but Harley Earl, GM's styling chief, insisted that it be carried over. For 1954 it was moved to the Century series, small chrome fins were mounted atop the rear fenders, and the wheel openings were elongated. Only 836 '54s were produced.

The Buick Skylark and its Cadillac Eldorado and Oldsmobile Fiesta stablemates were the progenitors of the large personal luxury cars that would later be exemplified by such models as the 1958 Ford 4-seater Thunderbird and 1963 Buick Riviera. And although Buick would revive the Skylark name a few years later, to most Buick enthusiasts, the only "real" Skylark is that first almost hedonistic 1953 model.

CADILLAC AND TAILFINS

Following the Second World War, Harley Earl, GM's colourful styling chief, decided that Cadillac needed a more distinctive rear end appearance. And his ideas would complement an era in which society was enthraled with rockets and jets.

Earl had been captivated by the look of the twin-tailboom stabilizers on the P-38 Lockheed Lightning fighter airplane that he and his stylists saw in the early 1940s. They decided to carry the idea over into GM's car styling, but with the wartime shutdown of auto production from 1942 to 1945, it took them until 1948 to realize their tailfin dream.

When the P-38-inspired tailfins appeared on the 1948 Cadillac they were really little more than raised taillights, with the fuel filler concealed

Cadillac introduces tailfins in 1948

under the left one. But after some initial hesitation, the public was captivated by them. They gave the rear of the car as well as the front its own distinctiveness, and the tailfin quickly became Cadillac's styling signature.

Inspired by Cadillac, tailfins proliferated, but remained reasonably restrained until 1957. That's when the Chrysler Corporation fired a styling shot across Cadillac's bow by introducing tailfins that were bigger and higher than anything on GM's finest. While Chrysler claimed that its 1957 fins reduced steering correction by as much as 20 percent, the real impetus, *a la* Cadillac, was styling, not vehicle stability.

Lincoln, still smarting from the market failure of its beautiful Continental Mark II, was intent on taking an increasing chunk out of Cadillac's luxury market. It too brought out huge, canted fins for 1957; they made the Cadillac's fins look puny.

The tailfin war was on, and Cadillac, the inventor of the fin as styling cue, was not about to be outdone. Under the aegis of Cadillac stylist Bill Mitchell, a student of Earl's, the stylists set to work to recover the fin crown. The result came in the 1959 Cadillac. Its fins were towering and pointed, and housed the taillights in two jet-like pods. It clearly re-established Cadillac as the king of fins.

While Harley Earl and the rest of the industry used tailfins strictly as a styling feature, they should not be totally trivialized; they can have a far more serious application. Properly designed tailfins can have a stabilizing affect on cars in cross winds. This was demonstrated by pioneering studies done in the 1930s by Professor Wunibald Kamm at the Motor Vehicle Research Institute in Stuttgart, Germany.

In a cross wind a car is subjected to pressure that acts to deviate it from its intended path. Direct head and tail winds have no affect. The higher the car's speed, and the more aerodynamically slippery its body is, the more it will be affected by cross winds. The wind pressure acts on a point called the centre of pressure, and the farther the centre of pressure is from the car's centre of gravity, the greater will be the car's susceptibility to cross winds.

If the centre of pressure is ahead of the centre of gravity, the car's nose will be pushed more than its tail, and the car will be inherently unstable because it will not tend to return to its original path. If, on the other hand, the centre of pressure is behind the centre of gravity, the rear of the car will be pushed more than the front, and it will be inherently stable because it is tending to return to its original path. Tailfins help counter this force by moving the centre of pressure toward the rear of the car, that is closer to the centre of gravity, thereby improving its inherent stability.

Rear engined cars such as the Volkswagen Beetle and the Chevrolet Corvair are particularly susceptible to cross winds because they have some 60 percent of their weight in the rear. The tall "sail area" provided by the rear engined Volkswagen van, for example, makes it a real handful to drive on a windy day.

This rearward weight bias results in the centre of gravity of the vehicle being quite far back. With the centre of gravity considerably behind the centre of pressure, the vehicle is inherently unstable. Fins would help cars like the Corvair and the Beetle some, but to be really useful they would have to be so large they would be impractical.

Dr. Kamm did extensive aerodynamic experimenting on automobiles, and is best know for espousing the use of an automobile body with a sharply cut-off rear end, resulting in the familiar flat-back shape seen on so many cars. It proved to be the most efficient and practical aerodynamic form for a car, and he became so associated with it that it is known as the "Kamm-back."

Kamm also did significant work with stabilizing fins. This culminated in the development of a car with large, vertical fins mounted high on the rear of the sloping roof. They resembled airplane rudders, and although they appeared as two fins, there were actually four. Dr. Kamm found that by dividing each fin with a vertical gap partway back, and splaying the rear fins out at an included angle of three degrees from the vertical plane of the vehicle, was the most effective use of fins.

Dr. Kamm was able to drive this experimental four-fin car at a right angle through an airplane's pro-wash without disturbance, while normal con-

1959 Cadillac tailfins

temporary cars subjected to the same condition suffered strong deviations in directional stability.

Tailfins have been used effectively for stability on land speed record cars such as Sir Malcolm Campbell's Bluebird Special which set a new record of 301.13 mph (484.6 km/h) on Daytona Beach in 1935. They were also used following the

1959 Cadillac Eldorado convertible

Second World War on a Fiat-powered, Pininfarina-designed record car, on Renault's "Shooting Star" record car, and on others.

To be effective as stabilizers, tailfins have to be vertical, not horizontal or slanted. Thus the flaring, horizontal fins on the 1959 Chevrolet, for example, or the canted blades on the 1959 Buick, would have no impact on directional stability. They were just appearance items.

The function of such aerodynamic add-ons as rear wings and front airdams that are found on both racing and road cars should not be confused with tailfins. Airdams and spoilers are intended to prevent lift at high speeds, not add directional stability,

as can be achieved with effectively designed tailfins.

While the fins used by Detroit, and some others, in the 1950s and early 1960s could have had some stabilizing affect - Chrysler's noted 20 percent steering correction claim may have been valid - they were used for style, not aerodynamics. After Cadillac's fins reached their extreme height in 1959, they began to recede. By 1965 Cadillac's fins would be gone. They soon died out in the industry.

Unfortunately the somewhat frivolous use of tailfins for ornamentation by Cadillac and others has overshadowed the much more consequential role they can play as vehicle stabilizers.

CHEVROLET CORVETTE STING RAY
1963–1967

Until the Dodge Viper appeared in 1993, the Chevrolet Corvette was North America's only genuine, homegrown sports car. It made its debut as a General Motors dream car at the Motorama show held in New York in January, 1953, and received such an outstanding response that GM decided to put it into production.

The Corvette had a couple of enthusiastic men in its corner: GM's chief stylist Harley Earl, and Chevrolet chief engineer Ed Cole. Cole was a dyed-in-the-wool sports car enthusiast, having owned a Jaguar XK120 and a Cadillac-Allard. He couldn't wait to get Chevrolet into the sports car business.

The target date for the first cars was June, 1953. Such a tight schedule didn't allow enough

1966 Chevrolet Corvette Sting Ray, performance and beauty

time to develop metal stamping dies, so it was decided to make the two-seater roadster's body out of glass-reinforced plastic, known generically as fibreglass. Bodies were built by the Molded Fiber Glass Co. of Ashtabula, Ohio.

It was planned to switch to steel later, but fibreglass quickly became a Corvette trademark and the bodies have been made of that material ever since. Kaiser-Frazer was working on its Kaiser Darrin sports car at the same time, also with a fibreglass body, but Chevrolet beat it to the punch. The Kaiser Darrin would last only a couple of years, until K-F went out of the automobile business in North America in 1955.

The Corvette running gear was based on modified Chevrolet sedan components. The wheelbase was shortened 229 mm (9.0 in.) to 2591 mm (102 in.), and the engine was set back 178 mm (7.0 in.) and lowered 76 mm (3.0 in.). This gave the car better weight distribution and a centre of gravity that was only 457 mm (18.0 in.) above the ground.

Power came from a modified version of the Chevy "Blue Flame" overhead valve 3.8 litre (235 cu in.) inline six. Such modifications as three horizontal Carter carburetors (to fit under the lower hood), twin exhausts, and a high-lift camshaft raised horsepower from 115 to 150.

Although it looked like a sports car, and was inspired by such British cars as the Jaguar XK120, those early Corvettes were more like sporty touring cars than real sports cars. They came, for example, with only a 2-speed automatic transmission.

It didn't take Chevrolet long to improve it, however. Under the guidance of Corvette engineer, later chief engineer, Zora Arkus-Duntov, who came on the scene almost at the beginning of its development and went on to become the "Father of the Corvette," this American sports car soon became worthy of the title.

The remarkable 1955 overhead valve Chevy V-8 (which would become known as the "small-block" engine) soon found its way into the Corvette. A three-speed manual transmission became available late in 1955, and by 1957 it could be had with a genuine all-synchromesh four-speed manual. Optional fuel injection appeared in 1957, and displacement was raised to (4.6 litres) 283 cu. in.).

Recognizing that it had a vehicle with some real performance potential, Chevrolet began working on competition versions of the Corvette.

These included the mid-engined CERV 1 (for Chevrolet Engineering Research Vehicle, a neat way to camouflage a racing car!). Also developed were the Corvette SR and SS series, and the Corvette Sting Ray racer.

The Sting Ray racer was the most significant of these for our story. Under the aegis of GM's chief stylist, Bill Mitchell, it grew out of a stillborn project known as the Q-Corvette, a car that was to have had its transmission and differential, called a transaxle, mounted in the rear.

The Sting Ray racer emerged in 1959 and closely predicted the styling of the production Sting Ray of 1963.

The 1963 Sting Ray was, except for the engine and transmission, virtually an all-new Corvette. The X-member frame was replaced by a wider, ladder-type unit with five crossmembers, and the over-all dimensions of the car were reduced.

The wheelbase was 102 mm (4.0 in.) shorter at 2490 mm (98.0 in.), the length of the car was reduced 35 mm (1.4 in.), width was down by 20 mm (0.8 in.), and height was decreased 61 mm (2.4 in.).

All of this made it a trimmer, tauter sports car, although the weight, at just over 1361 kg (3000 lb), was approximately the same as the previous model.

The most advanced feature of the Sting Ray was the new independent rear suspension. Based on the CERV 1, it had double jointed half-shafts which also functioned as the upper control arms.

For space reasons springing was accomplished using a lateral multi-leaf spring rather than the CERV 1's coils. It was a piece of engineering elegance, and the first modern American use of a fully articulated rear suspension system. The 1962 Pontiac Tempest had used independent suspension with a rear transaxle, but it used swing axles much like the early Volkswagens and Corvairs. The Tempest's rear axles were not fully articulated using two universal joints each.

Corvettes had always been open cars, but for 1963 a fastback coupe was added to the lineup. Its split rear window became an instant identifier for the '63, and made it a favourite collectible. By '64 it was gone, and some owners of '63s had the separating bar removed, much to their chagrin later when they discovered how valuable that '63 split-window was.

The styling of the Sting Ray, the second generation Corvette, was a distinct break from the previous rounded shape. A sharp character line now extended all the way around the car at wheel-top level. The headlamps were concealed behind electrically operated doors. The side windows were curved, and cowl-top ventilation was added. Although the trunk capacity was greater, unfortunately for convenience the trunk lid was eliminated; access to the luggage compartment was now gained by tilting the seat forward.

Power for the Corvette came from a 5.4 litre (327 cu in.) V-8, an enlargement of the 4.6 (283). There were four horsepower ratings: 250, 300, 340 and 360. Both automatic (still a 2-speed) and 3- and 4-speed manual transmissions were available, although the automatic was confined to the lower powered engines. And this year an alternator replaced the generator, and closed crankcase ventilation was fitted.

Performance, particularly with the higher

powered engines, was prodigious. *Road & Track*, in its October, '62 test, reported a zero to 60 mph (96 km/h) acceleration time of 5.9 seconds, zero to 100 (161) in 16.5, and a top speed of 142 mph (229 km/h) with the 360 hp, four-speed version. Fuel economy was not the Corvette's forte, however, with 12 to 15 mpg not unusual.

Over its five-year history the Sting Ray remained substantially unchanged, although it did receive some styling cleanups and performance enhancements. In 1965 a big-block 6.5 litre (396 cu in.), 425 hp engine made its appearance, as did four-wheel disc brakes. This was also the last year for fuel injection, although it would reappear in electronic form in 1982.

For 1966 the engineers bored the block out to 7.0 litres (427 cu in.), but still kept the horsepower rating at 425.

On all counts the Sting Ray was a winner. It was a styling success, had outstanding performance, and by Corvette standards, sold very well. Sales of the '63 totalled 21,513 compared with 14,531 of the '62s, and the Sting Ray reached its peak sales year of 27,720 in 1966.

The 1963 – 67 Sting Ray was a major departure from the earlier Corvettes. Although it was the shortest lived of all the Corvette generations, to many enthusiasts it was the high water mark in Corvette history.

It was sought after when it was new, and remains a desirable collectible, particularly the '63 split-window coupe. Although the Stingray name (as one word) would continue in the restyled Corvette, after a hiatus of one year, to many the only "real" Sting Ray was the 1963-67 model.

CHRYSLER'S TURBINE CARS

In the more than 100 years of automotive history, many attempts have been made to replace the internal combustion reciprocating piston engine. Although steam and electricity tried to challenge it in the early part of the century, neither was successful. In spite of a wide variety of engine configurations that were tried, only Felix Wankel's rotary piston engine, which came along in the 1950s, managed to gain a toehold in the market. This came about through an intense and tenacious development effort by Japan's Mazda, particularly engineer Kenichi Yamamoto.

1963 Chrysler Turbine, brave technological experiment

Attempts were also made by the turbine engine, and they came from several manufacturers, most notably Chrysler and Rover. Rover had worked with Rolls-Royce on turbine aircraft engines during World War II. After the war it continued its turbine experiments in automobile applications, and showed its first prototype turbine car in 1952.

The performance of the Rover "Jet" was outstanding. According to *Road & Track* magazine's June 1953 test, it could accelerate to 60 mph (96 km/h) in 6.5 seconds, to 100 (161) in 13.2, and reach a top speed of 151 mph (243 km/h). This was in a era when the Jaguar XK120, which could sprint to 60 (96) in 10 seconds, and reach a top speed of 120 mph (193 km/h), was considered a very fast car. Rover did considerable gas turbine development work, but was not successful in bringing one to market.

Chrysler had done military work during WW II on a V-16 piston aircraft engine which recovered some of the exhaust heat normally lost by using it to drive a turbine geared to the crankshaft. Although it didn't go into production, the resulting expertise helped Chrysler obtain a U.S. Navy contract after the war to develop a turbo-prop aircraft engine.

This contract ended in 1949, but Chrysler's George Huebner, a turbine experimental engineer, wanted to continue working on turbines. He still remembered his contact in the 1930s with General Electric's Dr. Sanford Moss, the acknowledged father of exhaust turbine driven superchargers, or turbochargers. During a demonstration of a turbocharged Chrysler car, Moss had encouraged Huebner to develop a turbine engine suitable for a passenger car.

Such a project seemed to hold a lot of promise because a turbine has many advantages over a piston engine. A turbine in effect replaces the pistons with a large wheel with blades around its periphery. This is rotated by a stream of hot gas flowing from continuous combustion, and power is developed in one vibrationless, rotary flow, not the start-and-stop reciprocating motion that pistons go through. It is lighter than a piston engine, has fewer parts, requires no cooling system, and can burn practically any kind of hydrocarbon fuel.

There are also disadvantages. The turbine spins very fast, in the order of ten times that of a piston engine's crankshaft, so must be geared down. Also, it runs high internal temperatures and generates a large volume of hot exhaust gases which must be dealt with. These high temperatures require rather exotic, and expensive, materials. And a turbine is much happier running at a constant speed, a condition seldom found in automotive applications, although perfectly applicable to aircraft use. Of particular significance for cars was the turbine's poor fuel economy, lack of compression braking, and high emissions of oxides of nitrogen (NOx).

Chrysler began its work on an automotive turbine in 1950, and was able to unveil its first generation turbine engine in 1954. It was installed in a 1954 Plymouth, and as well as being shown to the public, took part in the opening ceremonies of Chrysler's new proving ground in Chelsea, Michigan.

This '54 Plymouth demonstrated that Chrysler had made good progress in dealing with exhaust heat and fuel consumption. It turned out that the two were related. Passing the exhaust through a rotating heat exchanger (like a radiator) not only cooled the exhaust, but recovered heat that could be used to raise the temperature of the incoming charge, which improved fuel economy.

This '54 was followed by a second prototype, a 1955 Plymouth turbine car which was used for engineering evaluation. By 1956 Chrysler was ready to take its show on the road.

Chrysler installed a turbine in a '56 Plymouth and sent it on a 3020 mile (4862 km) trip from New York to Los Angeles. In elevations ranging from sea level to 7700 feet (2347 m) it was almost trouble-free, averaged 40 to 45 mph (64 to 72 km/h), and got 13 to 14 miles per U.S. gallon. This rate of fuel consumption was a disappointment, and Chrysler did a lot more development work, particularly with hotter running turbines, before showing its next one publicly in 1959.

That was a refined turbine installed in a 1959 Plymouth. In a 1200 mile (1932 km) trip from Detroit to Princeton, New Jersey it averaged a much more acceptable 18 miles per U.S. gallon. Chrysler was on the right track.

Over the next three years the engineers built several more turbine powered test cars and trucks, continually developing the turbine with such improvements as variable angle blades, which gave better acceleration and some engine braking. They finally felt ready to test their turbine in the hands of ordinary motorists.

In 1963 Chrysler built a fleet of 50 turbine cars. These had unit construction and were designed by Chrysler's chief stylist Elwood Engle, recently arrived from Ford. The bodies were built by Ghia of Italy. Not surprisingly, the 2-door hardtops bore quite a resemblance to the Ford Thunderbird. An interesting styling feature was the simulated turbine wheel surrounding the headlamps. At the rear, the taillamps were deeply recessed and the backup lights were set in turbine inspired projections. The turbine motif was carried through in the interior, which even had a cylindrically shaped console.

Other than the turbine inspired styling, and the gas turbine under the hood, the turbine cars were pretty conventional, even to the extent of using coil spring front suspension rather than Chrysler's torsion bars. With a wheelbase of 110 in. (2794 mm) and an overall length of 201.6 in. (5121 mm), the turbine cars were slightly smaller than the Ford Thunderbird.

The real world driving tests began in the fall of 1963 and ended in January 1966. In the process 203 randomly selected drivers covered 1.1 million miles (1.7 million km) under a wide variety of conditions.

The turbine cars proved to be quite mechanically trouble-free, with the majority of drivers praising the "turbine-like" smoothness and quietness, and the excellent cold weather starting. The main criticisms were acceleration lag and poor fuel consumption, although the turbine could use cheap fuel, such as kerosene.

With more development the future looked good for the turbine car. Chrysler went through several more generations, and the company even received a government grant to explore further developments in fuel consumption and emissions compared with the piston engine.

Alas as the 1970s unfolded the whole automotive environment changed. The first oil crisis in 1973 focused attention on fuel economy, and the public began clamouring for smaller cars and even diesel engines. Also, air quality concern was growing, and the government was formulating laws to cover both automobile economy and emissions.

Events were simply overtaking whatever chance the turbine car may have had of catching on. Its relatively high fuel consumption and NOx emissions were severe handicaps. Also, as the end of the decade approached, Chrysler was becoming less and less able to afford anything other than meeting economy and emissions standards, and developing vehicles that would save the corporation. Turbine work continued until about 1980 before it was finally abandoned.

Thus another potential challenger for the piston engine failed to live up to its early promise. And during all of this time, the old reciprocator, thanks in part to the application of electronics, continued to get better and better. Chrysler Corp., however, deserves credit for giving the automobile turbine a good try.

CROSLEY MOTORS INCORPORATED

Powel L. Crosley, Jr.'s Crosley Radio Corporation was the world's largest radio manufacturer in the 1920s; he even had his own broadcasting station, WLW in Cincinnati, Ohio. He manufactured home appliances and was an avid sports fan, owning the Cincinnati Reds, who played in Crosley Field.

But in spite of his love of baseball and his success in making a fortune in home appliances, Crosley had always cherished the dream of becoming an automobile manufacturer.

Crosley, born in 1887 the son of a Cincinnati lawyer, had an early interest in cars. As a teenager he built a home-made electric car. In about 1907 he tried to establish his own company to build a car called the Marathon Six. The venture was short-lived, and it's doubtful that any cars were made.

In 1913 he attempted to launch a light, tandem two-seater runabout called the DeCross. Unfortunately the cyclecar craze ended before production started. Probably no more than one prototype was built.

After studying engineering and law at the University of Cincinnati, Crosley eventually prospered in advertising. An interest in radios was sparked when he discovered that a crystal set for his 9-year old son was priced in excess of $100. Surely, he reasoned, there was a vast market for inexpensive radios.

Working with University of Cincinnati engineering students, Crosley developed a $20 radio. He formed the Crosley Radio Corp. to make the first mass produced, low cost radio. By the early 1920s Crosley was the largest radio manufacturer in the world.

Crosley added other appliances; his Crosley Shelvador refrigerator was the first to have shelves in the doors, an idea he purchased from a private inventor.

By the late 1930s a financially secure Crosley could again pursue his automobile dream. In spite of his six-foot-four-inch (1930 mm) stature, he believed in a minimalist approach to cars, the light runabout DeCross philosophy brought up to date. Even the imminent failure of the only other American manufacture of ultra-small cars, American Bantam of Butler, Pennsylvania, failed to daunt him.

Crosley's engineers designed a 2-door, 4-passenger car that was only 120 inches (3048 mm) long. It had an 80 inch (2032 mm) wheelbase, a 40 inch (1016 mm) track, and weighed just 925 pounds (420 kg). It was powered by a 15 horsepower two cylinder, 39 cubic inch (0.6 litre), air-cooled, engine from the Waukesha Motor Co. of Waukesha, Wisconsin.

To keep the price at $250, the Crosley was very basic; the seats were fabric over metal tube framing, the windshield wiper was hand operated, sound insulation was minimal, and it had sliding windows.

The Crosley was also spartan mechanically. There were, for example, no universal joints in the driveline; the rubber motor mounts were supposed to absorb any deflection. The mechanical brakes were cable operated.

Crosley introduced his car at the 1939 New York World's Fair. It would be sold through Crosley dealerships, and Crosley's appliance stores where the miniature cars would pass right through the front door. By year's end just over 2000 had been sold.

Mechanical problems soon surfaced, principally due to the lack of universal joints. In spite of the addition of a station wagon, pickup truck and van, 1940 sales slipped to just 422 units.

Crosley engaged a new chief engineer named Paul Klotsch who added universals, improved the motor mounts, and increased engine durability. This revived sales, and by the time World War II closed down the American auto industry early in 1942, Crosley had produced over 3300 more vehicles.

All car companies, including Crosley, participated in war work. One of the Crosley-built items was a small, sheet metal engine used to operate navy electrical generating sets. It had been invented by a Californian named Lloyd Taylor, and with an eye to his post-war plans, Crosley obtained the patent rights.

When peace came in 1945 Crosley returned to automobile building in earnest. He sold controlling interest in the radio and appliance part of the business, but kept the Reds baseball club and the automotive division. Crosley Radio Corp. became Crosley Motors Inc., with the head office in Cincinnati and the plant in Marion, Indiana.

His new engine was radical for its era. The cylinder block was not traditional cast iron. Thin-walled steel tubes formed the cylinders, and sheet metal stampings were used for such components as the water jacket and intake and exhaust ports. These were spot welded, crimped and press fitted in place, then all brazed together with copper in a furnace. This COBRA (COpper BRAzed) engine weighed a feathery light 59 pounds (26.8 kg) without starter or generator.

It had a single overhead camshaft, and the bore and stroke were oversquare at 2.50 by 2.25 inches (63.5 by 57.1 mm). Displacement was only 44 cubic

1949 Crosley two-door sedan, too small, too soon

With the pent-up demand for new cars becoming satisfied, the seller's market turned around. But that was not Crosley's only problem; the engine had a serious flaw that hadn't surfaced in military service. The sheet metal parts were subject to electrolysis, and when corrosion ate tiny holes through the parts, coolant was lost or entered the oil with disastrous results.

Word of the problem spread rapidly. Engineer Klotsch quickly designed a new cast iron CIBA (Cast Iron Block Assembly) engine. This solved the problem, and iron blocks were retrofitted to many older cars, but Crosley's reputation had been tarnished.

1949 Crosley four-wheel disc brakes, unsung pioneer had a better way

In spite of this setback, Crosley produced more contemporary styling accentuating horizontal lines for 1949. Four-wheel "Hydra-disc" disc brakes were fitted, the first ever offered in a production car. Unfortunately they proved troublesome and Crosley returned to drums after a year.

inches (725 cc), and its 26.5 horsepower was developed at over 5000 rpm. The 5-bearing crankshaft ran in an aluminum crankcase.

With his engine requirement solved, Crosley had a new post-war car designed. The wheelbase remained at 80 in. (2032 mm), but the 2-door sedan was now 145 in. (3683 mm) long, and weighed 1150 pounds (522 kg). Production began in mid-1946 and by year's end a car-starved market had absorbed 4987 sedans, plus a handful of convertibles and pickups.

Demand rose to almost 20,000 in 1947, and to more than 28,000 in 1948, some 23,000 of them station wagons, making Crosley the largest wagon producer in America. It was Crosley's best year.

1950 Crosley Hotshot, miniature sports car

Crosley added a new sports car, the Hotshot, to the line in 1949. In spite of its tiny 725 cc engine and 26.5 horsepower, its 1100 pound (499 kg) weight gave it reasonably good performance. Tom McCahill of *Mechanix Illustrated* magazine (10/49) recorded a zero to 60 mph (96 km/h) time of 28.1 seconds and a top speed of 74 mph (119 km/h).

He later tested the Hotshot's successor, the Super Sport, which had a 10.0:1 compression ratio, and recorded a zero to 60 time of 19.7 seconds, and top speed of 77 (124 km/h). Its performance almost equalled the English MG which cost more than double the Crosley's $1000, and had a 76 cubic inch (1.25 litre) engine.

McCahill summed up the Crosley sports car as a "tin tub on wheels with a fine engine." Crosley engines and chassis became popular with builders of sports racing specials. A Crosley was even doing well in the 1951 LeMans, France, 24-hour endurance race until its generator failed.

Powel Crosley owned a farm, and saw the need for a small, versatile, Jeep-type dual purpose utility machine. The result was the tiny, 63-inch

1950 Crosley Farm-O-Road, work the fields or go to town

(1600 mm) wheelbase 1950 Crosley Farm-O-Road. It had six forward speeds and two reverse, and such options as a dump or pickup box, and dual wheels.

The engine problems and a changing market had resulted in just over 7400 sales in 1949. In 1950, despite the addition of the sports car and utility vehicle, sales slipped to about 6800. The signs were ominous. Although sales held even at 6600 in 1951, this was away below the break even point. Powel Crosley accepted the inevitable and closed the doors on his dream in 1952 after building just over 2000 '52 Crosleys.

Powel Crosley and his tiny cars had several strikes against them. Most North Americans were not yet ready for smaller cars. And even if they had been, Crosleys were just too small to be suitable for anything other than local errands. He died in 1961 at the age of 74. He had been successful in home appliances, especially radios, and with his beloved Cincinnati Reds, but not with cars. The tiny Crosley remains a small footnote in automotive history.

DeSoto
1929 – 1961

The DeSoto, a member of Chrysler's corporate family from 1928 to 1960, never really shone on its own. Like a steady middle child, the DeSoto was overshadowed by its more illustrious stablemates.

Walter Chrysler had risen from roundhouse sweeper to the managership of the American Locomotive Co. plant in Allegheny, Pennsylvania. He went on to become general manager of Buick, but left in 1919 out of frustration with the management style of GM founder Billy Durant. He was soon hired by Willys-Overland's bankers to rescue that faltering enterprise.

That task accomplished, in 1921 Chrysler took over the management of the Maxwell Motor

1932 DeSoto convertible coupe, beauty in the Depression

1934 DeSoto Airflow, Art Deco styling fails to make it

Corp. which had recently merged with Chalmers. By 1924 Maxwell was marketing a Chrysler-badged car, and by 1925 Walter Chrysler had turned Maxwell Motor Corp. into the Chrysler Corp.

Chrysler was anxious to become a full-line automobile manufacturer. In 1926 he attempted to add a mid-priced car, along with more plant capacity and a strong dealer network, by buying the Dodge Brothers company of Detroit. When the deal failed, Chrysler's engineers began designing a new intermediate car.

This car, to be called the DeSoto, was an up-graded version of the new low-priced Plymouth that Chrysler was also launching in 1928 to compete with Ford and Chevrolet. When Dodge's bankers unexpectedly decided to sell to Chrysler in 1928, it was too late to abort the DeSoto.

Chrysler now had two mid-price cars, so a place was made for DeSoto by discontinuing the lowest priced Dodge. This pecking order lasted until 1933 when DeSoto was moved above Dodge in price, to establish the corporation's long running hierarchy of Plymouth, Dodge, DeSoto and Chrysler, and occasionally Imperial as a separate marque.

The 1929 DeSoto had an outstanding first year with production of over 81,000 cars, setting an industry record that would last as long as the DeSoto name itself. The DeSoto has such sound engineering features as 4-wheel hydraulic brakes (a corporate feature), and a spirited 2.9 litre (175 cu in.) 55 horsepower high-compression, side-valve six cylinder engine.

In spite of the onset of the Depression, DeSoto's first year success encouraged it to add "America's lowest priced straight-eight" for 1930. But most buyers who could still afford new cars preferred engines of fewer cylinders. DeSoto discontinued the eight after only two years, and wouldn't offer one again until 1952.

With the Depression hurting the auto industry, DeSoto production fell to some 35,000 cars in 1930, and to under 30,000 in 1931. DeSoto's 1932s were re-engineered and restyled, carrying a handsome "barrel shaped" horizontal bar grille. It got a stronger X-braced frame, and the smooth "Floating Power" engine mounts pioneered by

Plymouth in 1931. In spite of these changes, deteriorating economics resulted in model year sales of under 25,000 DeSotos.

The next big breakthrough for DeSoto, shared with Chrysler, was the controversial, aerodynamic "Airflow" styling of 1934. It should have been an outstanding success. Its smooth, Art Deco lines carved through the wind, and partial unit type all-steel body construction made it exceptionally strong. Locating the engine over the front wheels cradled the passengers between the axles for a better ride, an innovation that would soon sweep the industry. And the wider body provided more seating space.

Unfortunately, delayed production spawned rumours of problems. Some questionable GM advertising attacking the steel body, and the controversial new styling, blighted the Airflow from the start. In spite of good engineering it would not recover. Because DeSoto had committed fully to the Airflow model – Chrysler had cautiously also kept the conventional design – DeSoto suffered the full brunt of the Airflow's failure. Model year sales slipped to under 14,000.

DeSoto retreated in 1935 by supplementing the Airflow with the traditional Airstream model, and dropped its Airflow altogether in 1936, followed by Chrysler in '37. Chrysler's "car of the

1942 DeSoto coupe, shutting its eyes for WWII

future" turned out to be the car with no future, and sent Chrysler Corp. into a conservative styling mode that lasted almost 20 years.

DeSoto gradually pulled out of the Depression, and styling evolved into more integrated shapes that, although Airflow inspired, were not as radical. Headlamps were incorporated into fenders that flowed more fully into the bodies. Running boards shrank, and by 1941 were covered by flared door-bottoms. Concealed headlamps appeared in 1942 for one year only.

Industry-wide sealed beam headlamps came in 1940, and new "Safety Rim" wheels that held the tire in place in the event of a blowout. A 1941 DeSoto option was Chrysler's dual range, semi-automatic Fluid Drive transmission. Although performance was slow, it was more convenient than the manual transmission, but not as advanced as the 1940 Oldsmobile's fully automatic "Hydra-Matic."

World War II was raging in Europe, and in anticipation of a wartime shutdown, DeSoto's 1941 model year sales reached almost 100,000. The production hiatus lasted from February 1942 to 1945, and DeSoto, like others, turned to war work.

DeSoto's 1946 models were revised '42s, although DeSoto made more changes than most. All fenders were new, with the front ones now flowing into reshaped doors. A new, prominent vertical bar grille and large wraparound bumpers were fitted.

DeSoto enjoyed the post-war boom, the reliable and sturdy DeSotos being particularly popular as taxicabs. By mid-1949, when the pent-up demand had been satisfied, the Chrysler Corp. was ready with its new post-war models.

Chrysler Corp., remembering the Airflow's market failure, styled its 1949 models with more staid and upright lines than other manufacturers. This was influenced by company president K.T. Keller, who had succeeded Walter Chrysler in 1935.

Keller's main concern was that passengers could easily enter Chrysler's cars while wearing a hat. This conservatism hurt sales, and in 1952 the

1956 DeSoto Adventurer, DeSoto's performance fling

Ford Motor Co., third in industry sales since 1936, leapfrogged Chrysler Corp. into second place behind General Motors.

In addition to stodgy styling, Chrysler was also slow introducing new engines. While Oldsmobile and Cadillac had modern short-stroke, overhead valve V-8s in 1949, Chrysler's new hemispherical combustion chamber "Hemi" engine didn't arrive until 1951. DeSoto had to wait until 1952 for its Hemi "FireDome" V-8 (a six was offered until 1954). A fully automatic transmission came in 1954, years after the competition.

DeSoto got the corporation's all-new "Forward Look" in 1955, and it immediately moved Chrysler back into the mainstream of automotive styling. This, along with Chrysler's sensational C-300 supercar, gave the corporation new life.

DeSoto joined the performance market with

1961 DeSoto, the end of the line

By DeSoto's 30th anniversary it was apparent that it was in decline. Having lost its exclusive assembly plant of 22 years in 1958, DeSotos were now being built on a Chrysler line, except the Firesweep model which Dodge assembled. DeSoto was being drawn closer and closer to Chrysler, and unfortunately for DeSoto, buyers usually opted for the more prestigious badge.

its limited edition, 2-door hardtop Adventurer model in 1956 powered by a 5.6 litre (341 cu in.) 320 hp V-8. It featured gold coloured wheel covers and accent trim, and had the corporation's new-for-1956 tailfins. Although less than 1000 were produced, the Adventurer moved DeSoto away from its staid "banker" image.

For 1957 Chrysler broke out with tailfins that soared higher than ever, and it proved that its engineering prowess was intact with the introduction of longitudinally mounted front torsion bars. Called "Torsion-Aire," this suspension provided a much improved combination of ride and road holding for these large cars. DeSoto also could be had with Chrysler's outstanding new 3-speed TorqueFlite automatic transmission.

All mid-range cars were under price pressure, and DeSoto was gradually being squeezed as Dodge moved up and Chrysler moved down. It was thus not really surprising when the Chrysler Corp. announced on November 18, 1960, that the DeSoto was being discontinued. Just over 3000 1961 models had been built. As a sign of changing times, the model that would break DeSoto's first year sales record was Ford's new compact 1960 Falcon.

The end had come for a Chrysler family member that had been steady if unspectacular for over three decades. Although Chrysler's middle child had weathered the Depression's shakeout, it couldn't survive the post-WWII contraction in the industry.

ELECTRIC CARS

Self-contained electric vehicles powered by on-board batteries have been with us for a long time. As early as the 1830s Thomas Davenport, a Brandon, Vermont, blacksmith, built and operated a small electric vehicle. In 1839 Scotsman Robert Davidson constructed an electric locomotive that he operated successfully. It was, in true Luddite fashion, destroyed by some locomotive engineers.

Vehicles that actually began to resemble automobiles arrived at about the same time as gasoline powered cars. Philip Pratt of Boston demonstrated an electrically powered three-wheel carriage in 1888, only two years after the operation of the world's first successful gasoline powered cars by Gottlieb Daimler and Karl

1899 Columbia Electric

Benz of Germany.

Electricity would become a popular automotive power in the late 19th and early 20th century. In fact the emergence of the automobile at the turn of the century saw three power sources vying for supremacy: the external combustion steam engine; the battery powered electric motor; and the internal combustion gasoline engine.

Steam, with the longest history, held some 40 percent of the U.S. car market in 1900.

Electricity, however, seemed to have a promising future, with sales almost equal to steam's, dominated by the Columbia car out of Hartford, Connecticut. In 1899 the Columbia Automobile Co. produced 440 electric cars, making it

125

North America's largest automobile manufacturer. Gasoline held the remaining 20 percent of the market.

The three power sources were distinctly different. Steamers were powerful and fast, but before the invention of the flash boiler they needed some time to generate steam, and they required a skilled operator. Gasoline engines were still cranky, temperamental and noisy, but had good potential. The electric, however, was silent and simple to drive, making it a particular favourite with women. Its disadvantages were the need for a heavy battery pack, and the limited driving range provided.

Canada came quite early to the electric scene; its first electric automobile was constructed in Toronto in 1893 for patent attorney Frederick Featherstonhaugh. Designed by a transplanted English electrician named William Still, and built in John Dixon's carriage shop at Bay and Temperance Streets, it was displayed at Toronto's Canadian National Exhibition in 1893. The jaunty little electric was used for many years by Mr. Featherstonhaugh, but unfortunately has been lost to history.

Electrics distinguished themselves in early speed contests. In a French hillclimb in 1898 an electric driven by Belgian Camille Jenatzy averaged 29 km/h (18 mph), beating 56 gasoline and steam cars over the 1.8 km (1.1 mile) route.

This led to fierce competition between Jenatzy and another electric car driver, Count de Chasseloup-Laubat of France. It resulted in an electric car setting the world's first land speed record, established by Chasseloup-Laubat's Jeantaud electric at 63.3 km/h (39.3 mph) on December 18, 1898.

This was followed up a month later when Jenatzy and Chasseloup-Laubat met in a challenge race on January 17, 1899. Jenatzy achieved a speed of 66.6 km/h (41.4 mph), briefly setting a new record, until Chasseloup-Laubat upped it to 70.4 (43.7).

Jenatzy and Chasseloup-Laubat traded the record back and forth until Jenatzy's bullet-shaped electric finally triumphed with a mark of 106 km/h (65.8 mph) in Nice, France on March 29, 1899. It was the first car to cover a mile in under a minute.

Jenatzy's record stood for over three years until Frenchman Leon Serpollet reached 121 km/h (75 mph) in his Serpollet steamer on April 13, 1902. This ended the electric car's dominance of the land speed record. It would never again challenge the steam or internal combustion engined car's speed, although a modern electric, the "Spirit of San Antonio II," driven by Lloyd Healey, set a new electric car speed record of 331.7 km/h (206 mph) on Utah's Bonneville salt flats in 1996.

Following substantial market share at the turn of the century, electrics went into decline as the gasoline engine came under rapid development.

Metallurgy made giant strides, improved ignition systems replaced the crude "hot tube" method, and new oil discoveries in Texas made gasoline plentiful.

By 1905 the gasoline engine had some 86 percent of the market; electric and steam held about seven percent each. But while gasoline was destined to be the power of choice, electrics had made somewhat of a comeback by 1910.

Electrics were still the quietest and easiest to operate, and enjoyed renewed popularity for around-town use, particularly with the well-to-do. They were favoured by doctors and other professionals who disliked the noise, crank-starting and fumes of the gasoline engine.

The decisive blow to the electric car came, ironically, from an application of electricity itself. In 1912 the electric self starter was introduced on the gasoline engined Cadillac. Invented by a brilliant engineer named Charles Kettering, who would later become General Motors' chief of research, it freed the driver from the difficult and dangerous hand crank. Anyone could now operate a gasoline car.

Following the appearance of the electric self

1913 Detroit Electric

starter, electric car manufacturers began to disappear. The two longest survivors were the Detroit and the Rauch and Lang, later called Raulangs. Raulang lasted until 1928, and the Detroit Electric survived to 1938.

The longest lasting make, the Detroit Electric, began with William C. Anderson who was born in Milton, Ontario, and moved to Michigan as a boy. He founded the Anderson Carriage Co., in Port Huron in 1884. It moved to Detroit in 1895, and in 1897 went into the automobile field with the Detroit Electric. Anderson built 125 of these tiller-steered runabouts that year.

Anderson went to a closed car in 1908, called the Inside Drive Coupe. Detroit Electrics earned a reputation as well built, easy-to-drive cars, and production reached 400 in 1908, 650 in 1909, and 1500 in 1910.

In 1911 the company was renamed the Anderson Electric Car Co., and the cars were changed from chain drive to shaft drive from a centrally located electric motor. It was powered by banks of batteries under the "hood" and in the "trunk."

In spite of the fact that gasoline engines were now dominating, there were approximately 2000 Detroits built in 1914, and 3000 in 1916, boosted by the gasoline shortage of the First World War. The company name was changed again to the Detroit Electric Car Co. in 1919, but its prosperity was fading.

Detroit Electric built cars through the 1920s, but a declining market turned them to commercial vehicles. As the 1930s progressed it was building electric cars to order only, until the end came in 1938.

Electric car interest blipped in the 1950s and '60s with the surfacing of environmental concerns. The car was seen as contributing a significant share of air pollutants, and both Ford and General Motors announced electric car projects in the mid-60s.

Although electrics gained a renewed shot of interest with the oil crises of the 1970s, they were never a serious threat to the gasoline engine which by then was smooth, powerful and reliable. And thanks to the arrival of the catalytic converter and electronic powertrain management, and cleaner fuels, engines were emitting less pollutants with almost every succeeding model year.

Environmental concerns, led by worries over global warming, and the desire to conserve fossil fuels, rose again in the 1980s. As in the past, California took the lead, and the current movement was largely spearheaded by California's attempt to drive technology by forcing auto manufacturers to build zero emission vehicles (ZEVs).

In the early 1990s the California Air Resources Board set a standard which required all manufacturers who sold more than 35,000 cars per year in that state to make two percent of those cars ZEVs by 1998. This requirement rose to five percent in 2001, and to 10 percent in 2003. This standard was later relaxed when it became evident that it was impractical.

Although most manufacturers had electric car projects, General Motors was the most courageous in developing a pure electric. It showed its electric Impact car in 1990, and by 1996 was able to begin leasing its state-of-the-art EV1 to the public in selected warm climate areas of California and Arizona. The public response has been disappointing; there is still a great deal of scepticism among motorists over a car that offers the driving range of approximately two gallons of gasoline.

1996 General Motors EV1

With the gasoline engine a moving target, continually getting cleaner and more efficient, it appears that unless there is a dramatic breakthrough in storage battery technology, the pure electric car's future is dim.

Despite a steady but slow advancement in battery technology, the silver bullet – a light, cheap, powerful, long-lasting battery – has not yet materialized. The result is that the deficiencies that led to the electric's original demise, short driving range and high battery weight and cost, still plague it today.

What also must be factored into the equation, of course, is the pollution emitted by the usually fossil fuelled central power stations that produce the electricity used to re-charge the electric car's batteries.

With current technology, the best that electric power can probably hope for is to be paired with an internal combustion engine in a hybrid design, *a la* Toyota's Prius. Thanks to a very sophisticated computer-controlled power splitter that keeps the engine operating in its most efficient mode, the Prius's emissions and fuel consumption are substantially lower than a comparable gasoline car. And its engine/electric motor combination offers the driving range and characteristics of a regular car.

The Prius recently went on sale in Japan, where it is enjoying good sales success, and is scheduled to arrive in Canada in 2000 as a 2001 model. As we enter the 21st century, the goal of an acceptable pure electric car is still an elusive one.

FORD GT40

What is not very well known is that the original Henry Ford gained publicity for his fledgling car-building enterprises through racing and record runs. In fact he originally seemed more interested in racing than in building passenger cars.

His first company, the Detroit Auto Co., founded in 1899, failed after only 18 months. A second venture, the Henry Ford Co., was organized in late 1901, but Henry left in disgust when the principals brought in Henry Leland as a consultant. That company was reorganized and became Cadillac.

Ford then went into building and racing cars, and through the publicity gained was able to

1966 Ford GT40, America finally wins LeMans

assemble several backers, and the grand sum of $28,000, to found the successful Ford Motor Co. in 1903.

In the quest for publicity for his young company, Henry took his huge and brutal "999" racer out onto the ice of Lake St. Clair in January, 1904, and covered a mile in 39.4 seconds for a speed of 91.37 mph (147 km/h), fast enough to give Henry the world speed record (one hesitates to call it the land speed record), although it lasted only 10 days.

But Henry realized that he wasn't really cut out to be a racing driver, so he turned the job over to Barney Oldfield, the cigar-chomping road-burner who became an American racing legend.

Over the years Fords became associated with speed and racing, from Model Ts through Ford V-8s, which became the hot rodder's favourite. A team of Ford V-8 specials even ran in the 1935 Indianapolis 500-mile race. It was inevitable, then, that Ford would cross paths with the 24-hour race of speed and endurance that had been held in Le Mans, France, since 1923.

The 24 Hours of Le Mans is the most revered of all motor races. While the Indianapolis 500 is renowned as the biggest single sporting spectacle in the world, and the Monaco Grand Prix held in that sparkling principality is the jewel of the Grand Prix circuit, Le Mans is the best known of motoring competitions. Races have been held there since before the turn of the century, and it was the site of the first officially recognized French Grand Prix in 1906.

Throughout its long history the Le Mans 24 Hours had, until the 1960s, never been won by an American car, although Chrysler competed four times, finishing third and fourth in 1928, and other American cars such as Stutz and duPont also raced there. Many European racers, on the other hand, had won in America, including the Indianapolis 500.

In 1950, wealthy American sportsman Briggs Cunningham took two modified Cadillacs, one a box-shaped special, and the other a stock-bodied car, and finished 10th and 11th. This encouraged Cunningham to build his own sports racers in an attempt to win Le Mans in an American car, a cause he pursued for several years without victory; the best Cunningham finishes were a third in 1953 and a third and fifth in 1954.

Briggs would continue to drive competitively, but would enjoy more international success in another field: yacht racing. In 1958 he skippered the American yacht Columbia to victory in the Americas Cup.

In the early 1960s Lee Iacocca, general manager of the Ford Motor Co.'s Ford Division, was touting something called "Total Performance." In returning to racing, Ford was expending its vast corporate resources to contest the Indianapolis 500 and participate in stock car racing. It also wanted to round out the performance image of the company by buying Ferrari, the famous Italian builder of sports and GT cars. It was reportedly for sale.

Whether Enzo Ferrari was serious about selling, or just trying to goad Fiat into buying in, which they eventually did in 1969, or whether he got fed up with Dearborn bureaucracy, is not clear. Whatever the reason, the deal fell through after Ford had spent a lot of time negotiating. Ford felt snubbed, so it set out to show Mr. Ferrari that they too could build fast racing cars if they put their minds to it. The result was the Ford GT-40.

Ford felt that the best place to obtain expertise in building a world-class sports racing car was in Europe. They went to England and set up Ford Advance Vehicles headed by engineer Roy Lunn, an Englishman with extensive racing experience. They also engaged the services of ex-Aston Martin racing team manager John Wyer, and put him in charge of the racing program, and Eric Broadly, designer of the original Lola GT on which the GT-40 would be based.

Carroll Shelby, the legendary American racing driver who had retired due to heart trouble, was retained as a consultant. Ford Advanced Vehicles' orders, received in late 1963, were to prepare a Ford for the 1964 Le Mans race, which by that time was only 10 months away.

To speed up the process Lunn and group used the Lola GT car as the basis for the racing Ford, which was called the GT-40 (named for its 40 inch [1016 mm] height) and began adapting it to accept Ford components, a process that resulted in there being little of the Lola left. The style was developed in Ford's Dearborn studio, and aerodynamic testing was conducted in the University of Maryland's wind tunnel.

To link the GT-40 to Ford's road cars they wanted to use a domestic stock-block V-8, in this case the 289 cubic inch (4.7-litre) Ford Fairlane engine. Shelby had done a lot of development work and had turned it into a reliable and powerful competition engine. The question was, could a mundane American pushrod V-8 compete with the sophisticated, high-winding, overhead cam powerplants from the experienced racing stables of Europe.

Two of the mid-engined rear drive coupes were ready by the spring of 1964 and Iacocca introduced them at the New York Auto Show, saying that Ford's aim was to win at Le Mans. The scepticism displayed by many people at that time would soon seem justified; in June the three GT-40 Le Mans entries failed to finish the race.

The GT-40s were fast while they ran, however, with American driver Phil Hill taking his around at an average speed of 131.375 mph (211 km/h), the fastest lap of the race, and a new track record. But Ferrari won the race, and Mr. Ferrari smiled. But behind that smile was the knowledge that there was a formidable new presence at LeMans.

The following year Ford returned to Le Mans

with its GT-40s fitted with 427 cubic inch (7.0-litre) blockbusters used in National Association for Stock Car Auto Racing (NASCAR) cars, and turning out close to 500 horsepower.

Although the GT-40s, now built in Dearborn, were blindingly fast at 210 mph (338 km/h), they again failed to finish at Le Mans, although Hill did break his 1964 record with a 137.126 mph (221 km/h) lap. As in 1964 Ferraris were one, two, three at the finish, and Mr. Ferrari smiled again.

Lee Iacocca must have been doing a little cigar-chomping himself by this time, but the engineers and drivers persisted with more development and testing. In 1966 there was finally delight in Dearborn, vindication at last as GT-40s swept the first three places at Le Mans against the best that Europe had to offer. After more than 40 years an American car had finally won the 24 Hours of Le Mans. Mr. Ferrari frowned. Ferrari's six-year consecutive winning streak had been broken, and by Ford at that!

It would be the same story in 1967 when the new, lighter and more powerful GT-40 Mark IV again beat the Ferraris and Porsches at Le Mans, setting a lap record that would last until 1970, and average speed and distance records that

1967 Ford GT40 that finished 4th at 1967 LeMans

would stand until 1971.

Ford Motor Co. had proved its point, and decided to leave the international sports racing field. It sold the cars to John Wyer who continued to campaign them with the backing of the Gulf Oil Co. They went on to win Le Mans in 1968 and 1969, proving that their earlier victories had not been flukes.

In total, approximately 126 GT-40s were produced, and they allowed Ford to join the select group of marques, which includes Bentley, Alfa Romeo, Jaguar, Ferrari and Porsche, who had dominant eras at the mighty Le Mans.

FORD THUNDERBIRD 1955 – 1997

Ford developed the 1955 Thunderbird in response to North America's love affair with the sports car. This snappy two-seater was the answer to Chevrolet's Corvette which came in 1953, and stylish imports like XK-Series Jaguars and Austin-Healeys. After many iterations and 43 years, the Ford Motor Co. decided that 1997 would be its last model year.

The original two-seater Thunderbird was already suggesting its future direction. More civilized and luxurious than the Corvette, it had wind-up windows and big car amenities. Ford had taken the right market tack; first year sales swamped the '55 Corvette's by 16,155 to 674. But it remained a two-seater for only 1955, '56 and '57. Although popular and fondly remembered, almost to the point of being an icon, it was replaced by a four-seater in 1958.

Ford Division's general manager, Robert McNamara, had no gasoline in his veins. His decisions were based on cold business logic, and when he decided there was a limited market for two- passenger cars, that was the end of the little 'Bird. Enthusiasts could wail all they wanted to; McNamara's loyalty was to the bottom line.

Thus in 1958 the Thunderbird became a larger four-seater, launching a three-year styling cycle followed for many years. McNamara's prescience would prove correct. Besides almost doubling its '57 sales (37,892 vs. 21,380) in a recessionary year that saw only the T-Bird and the Rambler increase, those '58 Thunderbirds initiated a new personal luxury market segment. Although 'Bird enthusiasts never forgave McNamara, the four-seater would make more profit for Ford than Chevrolet made

1955 Ford Thunderbird, Ford's answer to Chevrolet's Corvette

from the Corvette, which stayed true to its two-seater beginnings.

The 1958 Thunderbird, known as the "Square-bird" for its angular styling, was a long way from the original. It was about two feet (610 mm) longer, 1000 pounds (454 kg) heavier, and had a wheelbase of 113 in. (2870 mm), which was 11 in. (279 mm) more than the '57. The '58 'Bird had unit construction, with the drive-train tunnel acting as a kind of rigid backbone. The 1936 Lincoln Zephyr had used a type of unit construction, but the T-Bird, and the '58 Lincoln Continental Mark III, employed a more modern form.

One of the results of unit construction was an ultra-low profile; overall height of the '58 Thunderbird was only 52.5 in. (1334 mm). This placed the driveshaft tunnel higher than normal, so the Ford designers turned it into a console which housed such items as the radio speakers and heater controls.

With such sales success, the '58 T-Bird went into 1959 little changed. Also, the 1960 was largely carryover, the main difference being a mesh grille. Sales of those '60 models boomed at about 91,000.

The Thunderbird was restyled for 1961, now nicknamed the "Roundbird" for its rounder, sleeker lines. While Ford called it "Unique in all the world," it shared much under the skin with the '61 Lincoln Continental. Dimensions were virtually identical to the '58 - '60 T-Bird, although

1959 Ford Thunderbird, more seats, more profits

the track was widened a little. The fifties-fad wraparound windshield was gone.

Among its features were a "Swing-Away" steering wheel that, Ford said, "...moves over to welcome you in." Of particular note was a convertible in which the rear-hinged decklid opened to allow the soft top to be stored. This kept the top out of sight, but swallowed up the trunk space.

To try recapturing some of the two-seater magic, the 1962 Sports Roadster had a fibreglass tonneau, including moulded-in headrests, that covered the rear seat. It was fitted with real wire wheels and knock-off hubs. As with previous models, this Thunderbird changed little during its three year run.

For 1964 the Thunderbird was restyled for its next three-year stint, combining influences of the "square" '58 - '60, and the "round" '61 - '63. The hood was lengthened and the body sides sculpted, but underneath it was not significantly different. Front disc brakes came in 1965, and due to shrinking demand, 1966 saw the last convertible.

In 1967 the personal luxury Thunderbird left the sporting end of the market to the Ford Mustang that had bowed in 1964 as a '65 model. For '67 the T-Bird expanded its lineup to include a four-door sedan on a 117.2 in. (2977 mm) wheelbase, 2.5 in. (63.5 mm) longer than the two-door. It did, however, maintain its long deck-short hood motif. Surprisingly, semi-unit construction returned with the body attached to a perimeter type frame using 14 mounting pads.

A minor restyling in 1970 brought a more sharply sloped rear deck and a prominent beak. Headlamps were exposed again after four years of being concealed. Mechanically the Thunderbird was largely the same as previously. The '70 T-Bird, along with the Continental Mark III, pioneered radial tires as standard equipment on American cars. The 1971s were little changed except for a toned down nose.

With the 1972 models the Thunderbird began its march toward its largest ever size. Now closely related to the Continental Mark IV, its more conservative styling rode on a 120.4 in. (3682 mm) wheelbase. It was 216 in. (5486 mm) long overall; this would ultimately reach 226 (5740)

by 1975-76. This generation stretched the T-Bird's styling run to five years with relatively few changes, bringing it through the first oil crisis that occurred late in 1973.

To rejuvenate sales that had been flagging for a few years, and prepare for 1978's fuel economy standards, Ford introduced a smaller, less expensive Thunderbird for 1977. Closely aligned with the Ford LTD II and the Mercury Cougar, length was back down to 216 in. (5486 mm), and wheelbase to 114 (2896). Styling was more formal and angular, and hidden headlamps were back. It carried through 1978 and '79 with few changes.

In 1980 the Thunderbird followed the industry to even more dramatic downsizing. Now based on Ford's new intermediate Fairmont, it was 700 pounds (318 kg) lighter and 16 in. (406 mm) shorter than the '79. Traditional Thunderbird styling cues such as the long hood-short deck theme and concealed headlamps were continued. Much more aerodynamic, its mechanical improvements included rack-and-pinion steering, electronic ignition and MacPherson strut suspension.

The Thunderbird went into 1981 little changed, although for the first time in its history fuel economy dictated something other than a V-8. A 3.3 litre six was the base engine. Little was changed for '82, except that the smallest engine was now a 3.8 litre V-6.

Nineteen-eighty-three saw a dramatically new Thunderbird, one that flew in the face of all

1995 Ford Thunderbird, the bird's last flight

it had stood for since the two-seater disappeared. It was taut, stylish, almost European, with a commendable coefficient of aerodynamic drag of 0.35. Downsized again, wheelbase was reduced 4.4 in. (112 mm) to 104 in. (2642 mm), overall length was down 2.8 in. (71 mm) to 197.6 (5019), and at 3200 pounds (1455 kg) it was 150 pounds (68 kg) lighter.

Engines were a 3.8 litre V-6 and a 5.0 litre V-8. Before the year was out they were joined by a 2.3 litre turbocharged overhead cam inline four from the Mustang SVO, producing the Turbo Coupe. There were few changes until 1987 when the T-Bird would again get a little smoother shape to carry it through to much bigger changes for 1989.

That's when the sleek Thunderbird Super Coupe appeared. In addition to regular V-6 Thunderbirds, the Super Coupe had a super-charged 210 horsepower 3.8 litre V-6. Although

it was a porky 3854 pounds (1748 kg), *Car and Driver* magazine reported a zero to 60 mph (96 km/h) time of 7.1 seconds, and a top speed of 143 mph (230 km/h). It was the fastest flying 'Bird yet.

It's interesting to note that during model years 1989 and '90 there were no V-8 engines available in the Thunderbird, the only time this would occur in its 43 year history.

The Thunderbird rolled on until 1994 with some appearance changes and powerplant options, but it was basically the same car. Then for 1995 it received restyled front and rear ends. Base engine was still a 3.8 V-6, supercharged in the SC. Ford's new 4.6 litre single overhead cam V-8 replaced the aging 4.9 pushrod V-8 as an option.

Little more development was done on the Thunderbird. The supercharged SC V-6 was dropped for 1996; in 1997 Ford announced that the Thunderbird was being discontinued.

The Thunderbird is gone but not forgotten. In its more than four decades it went from a two-seater to a four- and five-seater, and launched the personal luxury car market. It was powered by four, six and eight cylinder engines, and came naturally aspirated, turbocharged and super-charged. It was always rear-wheel drive.

The Thunderbird built up a lot of good will, so much so that it's a name too good to let die perma-nently. Don't be surprised if Ford's Thunderbird returns in the not too distant future.

Graham-Paige Motors Corporation

The Graham brothers, Joseph, Robert and Ray, and the companies they were associated with, covered a wide variety of activities and spanned almost the entire 20th Century. Starting out in the glass bottle business, they moved to the manufacture of trucks and cars, and ended up in the sports/entertainment field.

They were born to a prosperous Indiana farm family in the late 1880s, but eschewed the agricultural life in favour of other businesses. The discovery of natural gas in Indiana in 1901, combined with a ready supply of the right kind of sand, were the ingredients for successful glass manufacturing. A company called the Lythgoe Bottle Co. was formed, with Joseph Graham and his father as shareholders.

By the time he was only 19 Joseph had invented and patented a method to produce stronger bottles. Instead of the conventional way of blowing bottles, Joseph turned them upside down, thereby facilitating the downward flow of glass, and eliminating the thin, fragile shoulder-glass that then plagued bottle makers.

The Grahams, now with Robert aboard, took over the firm in 1905, renaming it the Southern Indiana Glass Co., soon changed to the Graham Glass Co. It prospered, and acquired the Loogootee Glass Sand Co. In 1916 Graham Glass became part of the Owens Bottle Co. of Toledo, Ohio, which in 1930 became the giant Libbey-Owens-Ford glass enterprise, with the Grahams still having a substantial interest.

Back on the farm following graduation from university, Ray Graham saw the need in agriculture for a light duty truck. He invented a kit to convert Model T Ford cars into one-ton trucks, and soon the three brothers were in the business of building truck bodies in Evansville, Indiana.

It was a short step to manufacturing complete trucks and buses, and by 1921 Graham had signed an exclusive deal with Dodge Brothers to supply them with commercial vehicles based on Dodge running gear. This access to an established name, and an extensive dealer network, led Graham to expand from Evansville to factories in Detroit, Stockton, California, and Toronto, Ontario.

By 1926 Graham Brothers, Inc., which had become the largest exclusive truck makers in the

1929 Graham-Paige

The Grahams quickly set about designing a new line of six and eight cylinder cars which they announced to the world at the 1928 New York Automobile Show. They featured such advanced engineering features as aluminum pistons, pressure lubrication, hydraulic brakes, and seven bearing crankshafts in the sixes.

Another unusual item was the 4-speed, "twin-top" transmission with, in effect, two high gears, one for spirited acceleration, and the other for easy cruising.

world, was absorbed by Dodge, now controlled by the bankers after the heirs sold out following the Dodge brothers' deaths in 1920. The talented Grahams became senior executives with Dodge, and were among its largest shareholders.

The Grahams were restless in an enterprise in which they did not have complete control, so they soon sold their Dodge interests and left the company. Although now out of the motor vehicle business, their interest in it remained. In 1927 they used their Dodge profits to buy the declining Paige-Detroit Motor Car Co., builder of Paige cars. They changed the name to the Graham-Paige Motors Corp.

These solid if unspectacular new Graham-Paige models jumped sales from just under 22,000 Paiges in 1927 to over 73,000 Graham-Paiges in 1928, a first-year industry record for a new marque. This turned a 1927 loss of $4.6 million into a 1928 profit in excess of one million dollars.

Nineteen-twenty-nine would see production rise to 77,000, although Graham-Paige slipped back into a deficit position because they had to dispose of an expensive company-owned dealership network at a huge loss. They returned to building commercial vehicles in 1930, only to be reminded by Dodge (now part of Chrysler), by way of a lawsuit, that the Grahams had sold their rights to build trucks for five years; G-P ceased making trucks in 1932.

The Depression progressed, and in spite of a wide range of good performing cars, sales slid to 33,500 in 1930. The Paige part of the car name was dropped in 1930, although most people continued to refer to them as Graham-Paiges. In spite of winning the prestigious Monte Carlo rally in 1929, posting many stock car speed records in Europe, and introducing the low priced "Prosperity Six," Graham sales fell even further to 20,428 in 1931.

Not about to take these losses lightly, G-P struck back in 1932 with its smashing new eight cylinder "Blue Streak Eight" model. It was styled by the famed designer Amos Northrup, and featured low, elegant lines, and a sloped, vertical-bar grille whose angle was echoed in the hood louvres and windshield slant. The radiator cap was concealed, and generous fender skirts hid the car's mechanicals. These valances would be the Blue Streak's most imitated styling feature.

Although the Blue Streak was sleek and fast – Cannon Ball Baker drove one up New Hampshire's Mount Washington in a record 13 minutes and 26 seconds – Graham-Paige sales declined to

1932 Graham Blue Streak

12,967 in 1932. It was all too depressing for Ray Graham, and tragedy struck the family when he committed suicide at the age of only 45, leaving Joseph and Robert to carry on.

In an attempt to rejuvenate interest after sales fell to only 10,967 in 1933, Graham-Paige introduced supercharging in 1934, its first use in a production car outside the exotic price range of such marques as Duesenbergs, Stutzes and Mercedes-Benzes. It boosted the eight's horsepower from 95 to 135, and the excellent styling and new performance helped raise sales to 15,745 in 1934, and to over 18,000 for 1935.

1939 Graham "Sharknose"

Under the financial pressures of the continuing Depression, Graham-Paige began using Reo Flying Cloud bodies in 1936, and now offered only six cylinder engines, although supercharging continued. Sales revived a little to 19,205.

In an attempt to make another dramatic styling statement as it had with the Blue Streak, G-P introduced its all-new "Spirit of Motion" model for 1938. With its prominent, forward leaning hood and fender line, and rearward sloping grille, it soon earned the nickname "sharknose." The rectangular headlamps were moulded into the leading faces of the fenders.

The sharknose, offered as a sedan only, had some interesting mechanical features. A hypoid rear axle eliminated the driveshaft tunnel, and the transmission hump was reduced by turning the transmission on its side. A "vacuumatic" gearshift used engine vacuum to assist the driver in changing gears.

Unfortunately for Graham, the sharknose was a sales failure, due in part to public apathy to its radical styling, and the onset of recession in an economy still trying to pull out of the Depression. With continuing losses, it appeared that G-P was just about out of the automobile business.

Graham-Paige managed to carry the sharknose into 1939, although largely unchanged. After only 6557 '39s were produced, the plant was shut down during the summer of 1939. It appeared that the end was imminent for G-P, but there would be a reprieve.

In a desperate move, an agreement was reached with the also faltering Hupp Motor Car Corp. in which G-P obtained the use of the old Cord 810/812 body dies which Hupp owned. In return, G-P would produce a car for Hupp using the Cord dies and a rear-drive chassis. It would be marketed as the Hupp Skylark by Hupp, and the Graham Hollywood by G-P, which also continued offering the sharknose as the Senior Graham model.

In spite of the fact that the Hollywood and Skylark were quite attractive cars, the project was doomed to failure largely because the dies were difficult and expensive to work with, causing assembly delays. After a few 1941 Skylarks and Hollywoods were built, production ceased in late 1940.

Graham-Paige then went into war production on government defence projects where it would finally earn it first profit since 1933. Then, as the Second World War was nearing an end, events would take a twist that would see G-P have one last fling in the automobile world.

Joseph Frazer was the man who would engineer G-P's comeback. Frazer was a veteran automobile executive who had worked his way up from a Packard mechanic to the general sales managership of Chrysler. In 1939 he become president of the troubled Willys-Overland Co. The famous Jeep would propel it back to prosperity during the war.

In 1944, after differences with Willys management, Frazer left the company, and with some

1941 Graham Hollywood

associates soon bought control of Graham-Paige. He announced that G-P would return to automobile production following the war, and it was to happen, but not as a sole G-P enterprise.

When peace came, Frazer joined forces with millionaire Henry Kaiser, famous for his huge construction projects and war-time production of Liberty and Victory ships. They formed a new automobile company called the Kaiser-Frazer Corp. Frazer's Graham-Paige Corp. was to contribute one-third of the capital in the form of building one Frazer car for each two Kaisers that Henry Kaiser made. Both were Graham-Paige designs.

The huge Willow Run ex-bomber plant near Detroit was leased from the War Assets Administration, and production of 1947 Kaisers and Frazers began in June, 1946. Alas, G-P resources were soon strained to the breaking point, and in 1947 the Kaiser-Frazer Corp. took over the entire car building operation.

G-P was out of the automobile business again, this time for good. It briefly turned to producing farm machinery, including the Rototiller.

Graham-Paige dropped the "motors" part of its name and became an investment holding company. Then in the early 1960s it entered the sports and entertainment business by acquiring New York's Madison Square Garden, and changed the G-P name to the Madison Square Garden Corp. Among other things it owned the New York Rangers hockey team, and the New York Knickerbockers basketball club. It was later absorbed by the giant Gulf & Western group.

Thus ended the saga of the Graham brothers in the automobile business. Robert died in 1967, and Joseph in 1970.

Intermeccanica International Incorporated

Vancouver based Intermeccanica International Inc. is Frank Reisner's brainchild. It's also a family business. Frank, is the president and guiding genius, his wife Paula, is secretary-treasurer, and son Henry, is vice-president. It builds replicas of 1959 Porsche Convertible D replicas, and Volkswagen's World War II Jeep-type Kubelwagen.

It's the progeny of an international stream of influences: a Hungarian-born, American-trained, Canadian engineer who honed his skills in Italy; a Porsche 356, product of a fine German automaker; and the entrepreneurial environment of Vancouver, British Columbia.

Henry, with the company since high school, oversees the day-to-day operation. He is intimately knowledgeable about the business, and very proud of what his father has accomplished.

Frank Reisner came to Canada from Hungary with his parents as a boy, and graduated from the University of Michigan in chemical engineering. A paint industry job brought him into the automobile business.

What started as a nostalgic 1959 European tour with his Czech-born wife Paula, turned into an odyssey spanning three countries – Italy, United States, and Canada – and four decades. Frank found Italy a delight for a car connoisseur, especially one with ambitions to build his own cars. The expertise was all there, the skilled panel beaters, the small fabricating shops, the component suppliers, and the enthusiasm. And Paula loved Europe.

Frank and Paula stayed to pursue a dream, and three months turned into 17 years. They established Construzione Automobili Intermeccanica in Turin in 1959 to produce such speed equipment as special intake manifolds, high performance camshafts, and Stebro exhaust systems for cars like Renaults, Simcas and DKWs.

Frank built one of the first rear-engine Formula Junior racers. Next came 21 little 500 cc aluminum rear-engine, two-seater technically advanced, high performance (100 mph; 160 km/h) coupes called IMPs (Inter Meccanica Puch), based on a Steyr-Daimler-Puch model.

With a solid reputation for high quality work, Intermeccanica's next car, the Apollo, was the

1969 Intermeccanica Italia

Intermeccanica also produced 10 high performance station wagons called Murenas for an American customer. They were powered by 7.0-litre Ford engines, and had every conceivable luxury and convenience item, including a bar. This was only one of Intermeccanica's many special low-production and one-off projects. By 1969 their reputation was such that three of their cars were displayed at the New York auto show.

Intermeccanica's next job looked like its big breakthrough. GM's German subsidiary, Opel, was impressed with the Italia, and commissioned Frank to produce a version fitted with Opel Diplomat running gear and a 5.7-litre Chevrolet V-8.

Called the Indra, it was a hit at the 1971 Geneva automobile show, and Intermeccanica produced 125 Indra coupes and convertibles by 1974. GM then severed its connection with Intermeccanica, and later developed its own version. Intermeccanica's former German distributor, Erich Bitter, sold it as the Bitter CD. It was a bitter pill for Frank.

Intermeccanica's future looked dim until it was learned that the City of San Bernardino, California, would assist in establishing a speciality

one that really launched Frank into car building. Intermeccanica produced the sleek two-passenger grand touring coupe and convertible Apollo bodies, then shipped them to a U.S. company which installed running gear and Buick aluminum V-8 engines, and sold them as Apollos and Griffiths. An Apollo was Best of Show at the 1965 New York auto show.

When the American business failed, Frank began completing the cars in Italy. He used Ford V-8 engines and running gear, and called them Torinos. When Ford objected, he changed the name to Italia, and by 1970 Intermeccanica had built more than 500 of them.

car building operation. Two Ford engined proto-type Indras were built and shipped, a deal was consummated, and Intermeccanica moved its tooling and cars to California in 1975.

Within a month of Frank's arrival in California with his wife and three children, the project was cancelled.

Undefeated, Frank set up a partnership with Tony Baumgartner, a Santa Anna, California businessman. The business, Automobili Intermeccanica, began producing Porsche Speedster replicas based on a prototype developed by Frank. It was so successful that from 1976 to '79 Automobili Intermeccanica produced some 600 of them. Baumgartner then bought out Frank's half-interest, and he was again at loose ends.

After considering a large neo-classic with Mercedes and Duesenberg styling influences, based on a Checker (of taxi-cab fame) chassis, Frank returned to his first love, Porsche. He developed another replica based on the 1959 356A Convertible D. This Speedster successor had such improvements as roll-up windows, a taller windshield for better visibility, and more comfortable seats.

Frank's former Montreal Italia importer, now living in Vancouver, urged him to build his new replica in Canada. He offered to invest in the enterprise, and Intermeccanica came to Vancouver in 1981.

The first Canadian-built Porsche replicas had shortened Volkswagen Beetle floorpans with an added sub-frame. "The pan," says Henry Reisner, "became the achilles heel of the vehicle – there was not much flexibility in what you could do."

Frank designed a tubular steel frame which was a stiffer platform for the body and torsion-bar-and-trailing-arm suspension. Shorter rear torsion bars allowed the engine/transaxle to be moved forward 75 mm (about three inches) for better weight distribution.

These frames are made of 3.0-in. X 5.0-in. (76 X 127 mm) mild steel rectangular tubing welded together in a jig. The side rails provide an efficient conduit for the heater pipes from the engine. Enclosing the ducts and boosting heat delivery with a three-speed fan results in comfort that would turn Beetle owners from their customary blue to an envious green.

The high quality, one-piece fibreglass body prevents cracking, creaking and flexing. Aircraft quality rivets attach it to the chassis, producing, in effect, a very rigid fibreglass-steel monocoque.

Volkswagen air cooled, horizontally-opposed (flat) overhead valve four cylinder engines from Brazil or Mexico are used. Standard is a 1.6 litre 75-horsepower version, with an 85-hp upgrade available. Those seeking more performance than the approximately 150 km/h top speed, and 12-second zero-to-100 km/h acceleration of 1.6 litres, can order a California-modified 2.2 litre with 130-plus hp.

1997 Intermeccanica Roadster RS, Porsche beauty revived

Roadster production out of the 5000 square foot working area is 25 to 30 cars per year. Four regular staffers, plus a few contract workers, do everything except mould the body and the final painting. All cars are built to order, with approximately 75 percent exported to Japan.

Because Transport Canada applies the Motor Vehicle Safety Act to his tiny company, Intermeccanica can't sell its cars outside British Columbia, although it can sell in many countries around the world, including all U.S. states, Japan and Hong Kong. Transport Canada has threatened Frank with fines up to a million dollars, and imprison-ment, if he sells cars across provincial boundaries. "They want to see us out of business," says Frank. "You can't fight city hall, right? and this is city hall for us."

At the urging of its Japanese distributor, Frank designed a replica of the World War II Volkswagen Kubelwagen, Germany's version of the Jeep. Although lukewarm about the project, Frank agreed, because, as he says, "the Japanese market is very important to us."

Kubelwagen production started in 1997, and they are priced at about $26,000. Roadster RSs are $32,000 to $41,000 depending on options

1999 Intermeccanica Kubelwagen

ranging from four-wheel disc brakes (front discs are standard) to an automatic transmission.

While countless hopefuls have tried to start a car company, Canadian Frank Reisner's success stands almost alone. While Intermeccanica's total production wouldn't match one day's output by General Motors, Frank's enterprising spirit, ingenious, uncompromising engineering, and personal drive have produced a legacy of wonderful specialty cars.

Those jewel-like Intermeccanica Roadsters and square-cut Kubelwagens roll out of Frank's little Vancouver factory, and into the hands of appreciative buyers around the world, except, of course, in most of Canada.

JAGUAR E-TYPE

The V-8-powered Jaguar XK8 coupe was unveiled at the Geneva Auto Show in March 1996, followed by the convertible version at the New York International Auto Show in April. Jaguar, owned by the Ford Motor Co., hoped the XK8 would revive the magic of the E-Type that bowed at Geneva in March 1961, 35 years earlier. But just to be sure that folks didn't miss the point, Jaguar called its new XK8 the spiritual successor to the E-Type.

The E-Type Jaguar was, after all, a stunner, as the fabled XK120 had been back in 1948. Also called the XK-E, its sensuous shape was inspired by the Le Mans winning C- and D-Types, and the short-lived production XK-SS of the 1950s. It combined race-proven performance, sensational styling, and road-going civility in one irresistible yet affordable package.

It was a spectacular success with the public, and the motoring press who afforded it universal praise. *Road & Track* called it "The sensation of the New York show. The car comes up to and exceeds all our expectations." *Car and Driver* named it "The most exciting sports car news of 1961."

The E-Type was due. By the late fifties it was becoming apparent that the XK series was reaching the end. Conceived in the forties, and passing through XK120, 140, 150 and 150S iterations, it had grown fat, heavy and obsolescent.

In preparing the XK's replacement, Jaguar drew on an amalgam of old and new components. The engine/transmission unit was carried over from the XK150S, giving the E-Type the famous Jaguar 3.8 litre double overhead cam inline six. It drove the rear wheels through a four-speed manual transmission and developed 265 horsepower at 5500 rpm.

1962 Jaguar E-Type roadster, stunning styling and performance

The front suspension was also inspired by the XK and C- and D-Types, using A-arms and longitudinal torsion bars. At the rear, however, Jaguar stepped out boldly, replacing the XK's solid axle with a chassis-mounted differential and independent suspension using two coil springs on each side. Braking was by four-wheel discs, with the rear ones mounted in-board flanking the differential for reduced unsprung weight. Steering was by rack-and-pinion.

The E-Type replaced the XK's traditional body-on-frame structure with a chassis/body that combined unit construction and space frame technology. From the cowl rearward it was unitized using stressed skin and box section rocker panels. From the cowl forward was a bridge-type structure fabricated from small, square tubes, and bolted to the main body. It carried the engine, suspension, etc. The result was a car that was strong yet light; at 1234 kg (2720 lbs), it weighed 200 kg (441 lbs) less than the XK150S.

All of this technology was clothed in a beautiful, windcheating body that was the work of aerodynamicist Malcolm Sayer. From the oval-shaped grille opening adorned by a single horizontal bar, the lines swept graciously back over sensuously sculpted fenders, around the passenger compartment, and continued on to a pertly tapered tail.

A hood bulge, necessary to make room for the tall engine, didn't detract from the overall impression that the E-Type, particularly the coupe, was carved from a single billet of steel. It rode on beautiful wire-spoke wheels with knock-off hubs.

It was the first Jaguar that wasn't styled by Sir William Lyons (he was knighted in 1956), the spiritual and literal father of the Jaguar. Whereas Lyons penned his designs from the heart, guided purely by aesthetics, and very successfully at that, Sayer approached it from a scientist's perspective. Both produced shapes that were milestones in automotive styling.

Although its wheelbase was only 2438 mm (96 in.), and overall length 4453 mm (175.3 in.), the E-Type's sleek form made it appear longer than it was. And to some eyes, the fastback coupe with its large side-hinged rear window-hatch actually looked better than the convertible.

As would be expected from a car of this weight, power and aerodynamics, the E-Type had prodigious performance. *Road & Track* magazine (9/61) reported a zero to 60 mph (96 km/h) acceleration time of 7.4 seconds, zero to 100 (161) in 16.7, and a top speed of 150 mph (242 km/h).

As good as that original 1961 E-Type was, changes were inevitable. In 1965 the engine was enlarged to 4.2 litres to cope with such demands as automatic transmissions, air conditioning and emission controls. A new fully synchronized four-speed gearbox was also fitted.

1967 Jaguar E-Type coupe, snug, fast, comfortable

This arrived with the 1971 Series III V-12, the final version of the E-Type. Although other marques such as Ferrari and Lamborghini used V-12 engines in exotic, limited production cars, Jaguar's V-12 would be the first mass production V-12 since the demise of the Lincoln Continental in 1948.

In contemplating a return to full scale international sports car competition in the 1960s, Jaguar had developed a mid-engined racer fitted with a double overhead cam V-12 developing over 500 horsepower. The racing project was shelved, but Jaguar's chief engineer William Heynes never forgot the charm of the V-12.

When a production V-12 was developed for the Jaguar, it would not be fitted with twin overhead cams, a somewhat surprising move in view of the racing engine experience, and the fact that double cams had been so successful on the XK six. Jaguar engineers felt, however, that the complexity and extra weight of twin cams were not warranted in a passenger car engine.

The Series III V-12 was an aluminum, single overhead cam design displacing 5.3 litres (326 cu in.). It originally developed 314 horsepower, but

In 1966 a 2 + 2 coupe was added by stretching the wheelbase 229 mm (9.0 in.) to make room for two small rear seats. Unfortunately, lengthening the body detracted somewhat from the purity of proportion that defined the lines of the two-seater model.

The Series II E-Type arrived in late 1968. Safety legislation had resulted in the headlamps being raised and their aerodynamic plastic covers being removed, as well as the fitting of side marker lights and larger bumpers. Emission hardware was also starting to take its toll on power, which prompted Jaguar to begin work on more horses for the E-Type.

1973 Jaguar E-Type Series III V-12 roadster, 12 cylinder elegance

to reach 60 mph (96 km/h) was the same as the original 1961 E-Type, zero to 100 (161) took almost two seconds longer at 18.5, and top speed had dropped from 150 mph (242 km/h) to 135 (217).

The Series III V-12 2 + 2 coupe was carried on until the fall of 1973, and the roadster until 1975. During the 15 year life of the E-Type some 72,529 had been built in all series.

The E-Type Jaguar's lines were so pure and ageless that the Museum of Modern Art in New York added a 1963 model to its permanent collection, only the third car to be so honoured; the others were a 1946 Cisitalia Gran Sport and a 1990 Ferrari Formula One Grand Prix car. In so doing, chief curator Terence Riley stated that the E-Type "...perfectly fits the criterion of a landmark design object."

Jaguar replaced the E-Type with the XJ-S in 1975. To many Jaguar enthusiasts, however, it wasn't a genuine replacement. They were still awaiting the "real" new E-Type; the XK8 could well prove to be it. In the meantime the E-Type is a much sought after collectible today.

by the time it had been desmogged to meet North America's pollution laws it arrived here with 250.

When the Series III V-12 made its debut at the New York Auto Show in 1971 it looked like an original E-Type on steroids. A cross-hatch grille had been fitted, the 2 + 2's longer wheelbase was now standard, and the fenders had been flared to accommodate the wider track and fat Dunlop E70-VR15 tires.

Once in the hands of the testers (*Road & Track* 10/72), it was apparent that while the Jaguar was still very quick, the impact of the big V-12 engine had been cancelled by added weight and pollution control equipment. The 7.4 seconds it took

KING MIDGET
MIDGET MOTORS CORPORATION

If you had been reading craft magazines like *Mechanix Illustrated*, *Popular Mechanics* and *Popular Science* back in the 1940s, '50s and '60s, you would have found tucked away among the advertisements for such technical wonders as Marvel Mystery Oil and the Original Whiz Saw, an advertisement for a little car called the King Midget. Billed as the "worlds's lowest priced 2 passenger auto," it promised that you could "drive it for 75 cents per week" while enjoying "amazing performance" and "surprising comfort."

The King Midget was America's entry in what came to be called the microcar class. Often referred to as "Bubble Cars," some had only three

1946 King Midget, boy racer

153

wheels. Such cars as Isetta, Messerschmitt, Heinkel and Bond were sold in Europe after World War II as economical replacements for a motorcycle and sidecar combination. Some were exported to North America, but the King Midget was the only American microcar that actually made it into production.

The King Midget was the brainchild of two World War II Civil Air Patrol pilots named Claud Dry and Dale Orcutt. They felt that the light aircraft principles of economy, low weight and dependability could be applied to a low-priced automobile. To pursue this idea they formed Midget Motors Manufacturing Co., later Midget Motors Corp., in Athens, Ohio, in 1945 to bring their idea to fruition. As well as being pilots, both men had built their own airplanes before the war, so they were skilled craftsmen.

After a period building motor scooters, Dry and Orcutt began production of their first King Midget cars in 1946. This version was a single-passenger model powered by a one-cylinder, six horsepower, four-cycle, side-valve, air-cooled engine. Wisconsin was the company's main engine supplier, although Kohlers would also be used. It was mounted in the rear, as the engine would be in all Midgets, and had chain drive to the right rear wheel. There was no reverse gear; to back the car up the driver had to get out and push!

Those first cars were really tiny and weighed just 330 pounds (150 kg). They had a wooden frame and were initially sold as kits, but were soon offered fully assembled. Although it looked somewhat like a midget race car, the claimed top speed of 50 mph (80 km/h) was hardly racing performance, but it would certainly have felt fast in a vehicle this small. The price was right at $100 in kit form, without an engine. There were no dealers; the cars were bought by mail order and arrived in a crate.

That Midget sold reasonably well, but it was too small to be really practical. The company, therefore, brought out its second-generation Midget in 1951. This was a two-passenger model with a folding canvas top and windshield, and although small, it looked more like a real car. It was bigger too, with a wheelbase of 72 inches (1829 mm), an over-all length of 96 inches (2438 mm), and a weight of some 500 pounds (227 kg).

In spite of its size, the King Midget had many full-size car features. The engine was equipped with a generator and battery ignition system, which meant it could be fitted with sealed beam headlamps and an electric starter (early ones had rope starters). Horsepower of this series two K-M was 7.5, later raised to 8.5.

In keeping with their aircraft background, Dry and Orcutt soon abandoned wood, and fitted the King Midget with a light but sturdy perforated girder and tubing frame. A factory demonstration proved that it was strong enough to support 20 men, yet light enough that it could be easily lifted by one man. Suspension was independent all around using oil immersed coil springs. Brakes were hydraulic, on the rear wheels only in early models, but on all four later; a handbrake operated on the rear wheels.

With its two centrifugal clutches that operated like a two-speed automatic transmission (early ones had only one speed), the Midget was pure simplicity to drive. One merely moved the small selector lever under the seat to drive, and stepped on the accelerator to go and on the brake pedal to stop. A reverse gear was now provided, also engaged by the lever.

The third-generation King Midget came out in 1958 and was even bigger. The wheelbase was up to 76.5 inches (1943 mm) and length to 108 (2743). Weight had increased to 670 pounds (304 kg).

Its 23 cubic inch (0.38 litre) Wisconsin engine developed 9.25 horsepower at a modest 3400 rpm; this was replaced in 1966 by a 12 hp Kohler. And, like all Midgets, it was extremely frugal on gasoline, figures of 50 to 75 mpg (U.S.) being typical.

Styling of the Midget's steel body was now much more angular, with some resemblance to an undersized Willys Jeepster. There was even a bit of space to carry items in a compartment behind the seat and a shelf under the hood. It ran on 5.70 by 8-inch tires.

In 1966 the King Midget's course took a different turn. Joseph Stehlin, Jr., an executive from England's Rootes Group was so captivated by the little car that he organized a consortium of businessmen which bought the company. Stehlin became president, and Dry and Orcutt were retained as consultants.

Better assembly management increased production from approximately 1-1/2 cars per day to four. But the King Midget didn't have a dealer network, and while the informal sales methods had been adequate for the lower production, they weren't for the higher output. A buildup of inventory and lack of cash flow forced the company into bankruptcy. An attempt to revive it with a fibreglass bodied commuter car that resembled a dune buggy failed.

The King Midget's small size seemed to present a challenge to many Midget drivers, and there are reports of them making what sounds like impossible trips. One was driven from Northern Michigan to Mexico City and return. Another was driven by a James B. Gilmer III from San Francisco, California to Atlantic City, New Jersey in four days, 11 hours and 21 minutes of driving time spread over seven days and three hours. Mr. Gilmer averaged almost 600 miles (966 km) per day, and covered a total of 3095 miles (4983 km). Total cost was $26.35 for gasoline, oil and greasing. Probably the most dedicated owner is a Mr. Norman Kendall who has driven his 1960 Midget over 115,000 miles (185,000 km).

1963 King Midget, boy racer grows up

Although the King Midget was too small to be considered a real car, it did have novelty value, not to mention outstanding economy. Enthusiastic owners still get together each August back in Athens, Ohio, where it all started, to swap tales and show off their Midgets. The main event of the day is the High Street Hill Challenge, a test of the ability to climb the original Midget factory test hill. Those that can't quite make it are given a friendly push by the spectators.

The King Midget was a footnote in American automotive history, but one that must be acknowledged. Estimates of total production vary from as low as 4000 to as a high as 14,000, but the figure most often quoted is about 5000.

In addition to its surprising production total, it also outlasted all other new American post-WWII automobile manufacturers. In the period following the war, the pent-up demand for cars had lured many new would-be automakers onto the scene. Names like Tucker, Davis, Playboy, Crosley (although it had built a few cars before the war), and Kaiser-Frazer tried to break into the industry. Some barely got past the prototype stage. Kaiser-Frazer, on the other hand, was able to survive and continue building cars in North America for 10 years, before succumbing to the competition in 1955. Crosley had a few good years and then went out of the car business in 1952.

While these upstart manufacturers were falling around them, King Midget managed to stay in car-building from 1946 to 1969. That in itself is a remarkable feat, especially with a tiny car that was well out of the mainstream. But perhaps that's the secret of its longevity; Dry and Orcutt had kept their expenses down and their production small, and tapped into a specialized niche market that was just different enough to attract a small but steady flow of customers.

T-Series MGs

The little English MG two-seater roadsters that began landing in North America following the Second World War were quintessential sports cars. With their cut-down, rear-hinged doors, folding windshields, classic square-cut lines, and floor-shift 4-speed transmissions, they represented a new, lighthearted approach to motoring, one that really involved the driver.

These were no prosaic, work-a-day Plymouths or Chevrolets; they were strictly for having fun. Their motto was "Safety Fast," and their trademark octagon-shaped badge soon became revered. There was even a dial on the instrument panel called a tachometer that displayed the engine's crankshaft revolutions. The MG started a whole new motoring cult.

The MG name dated back to the early twen-

1939 MG TB, "Spirit of Toronto"

ties when Cecil Kimber, manager of Morris Garages, sales arm of Morris Motors, customized and hopped up a Morris Oxford and named it the MG (for Morris Garages). That "Old Number One" evolved in 1924.

MG became a company in its own right (MG Car Co.) in 1928, and soon moved from Morris's Oxford location to establish a factory in the town of Abingdon-on-Thames, also in Oxfordshire. Several models were produced, and in 1929 MG built the first Midget, or M type, a fabric-bodied, pointed-tail roadster based on the overhead cam engined Morris Minor. MGs established an enviable competition record during the 1920s and thirties.

The first of the T-series MGs, the TA, came in 1936, a year after the takeover of MG by the Nuffield Group. The TA had many improvements over the P-series that it replaced, such as hydraulic brakes and a roomier interior. The overhead cam engine was replaced by a pushrod-operated overhead valve unit.

The TA was supplanted by the TB in 1939. While its appearance was similar to the TA, under the hood it received the new "XPAG" four cylinder pushrod engine. This had slightly less displacement – 1250 cc vs. 1292 cc – due to a shorter stroke and larger bore. Its dimensions were 66.5 X 90.0 mm (2.62 X 3.54 in.), compared with the 63.5 X 102.0 mm (2.50 X 4.02 in.) of the engine it replaced.

The shorter stroke allowed the engine to make up for its loss in displacement by revving to 5200 rpm compared with 4800. Other mechanical improvements included a counterbalanced crankshaft and a dry-plate clutch instead of the oil-immersed cork type.

The onset of the Second World War would soon curtail TB production. With less than 400 produced before the Abingdon plant was changed over to war work, it was the rarest of all the T-series MGs.

But rare or not, it was a tough little car that in spite of being bred for the narrow winding roads of England, would prove itself equal to the long highways of North America, even when it was 56 years old! In 1995 Andrew Patenall and Tim Bayley of Toronto, Ontario, entered their "Spirit

1948 MG TC, ignited sports car fire in North America

of Toronto," a 1939 MGTB, in the Great North American Race, a fun-filled rally that ran from Ottawa, Ontario, to Mexico City, Mexico.

They didn't win, but they had a wonderful experience as the tiny English roadster and its pilots met with warm-hearted good cheer everywhere, proving that the reservoir of good will for old MGs is wide and deep.

The first MG to come to North America in any quantity was the 1946-49 TC Midget model, a continuation of the T-Series MGs Following the Second World War, British manufacturers, as well as others, began offering pre-war designs until new models could be developed. Thus the MG TC evolved from the short-lived TB, with the body widened some 102 mm (4.0 in.) to provide more passenger space.

MG TC production started in November 1945 and they soon began trickling over here in small numbers, the first ones imported privately by returning servicemen.

Derived as it was from a 1930s design, the TC's engineering was pretty basic. Stiff leaf springs all around, and a solid front beam axle provided a ride that, even charitably, could only be described as firm. Its long-stroke 1250 cc overhead valve inline four – carried over from the TB – produced 54 horsepower at 5200 rpm. It pushed the TC to a rather modest 121 km/h (75 mph) top speed.

1953 MG TD, consolidated TC's beachhead

But the MG seemed to rise above its moderate performance. The TC had elegance and flair, and its quick steering and "busy" driving suggested far more speed than it had. It rode on big, 19-inch, wire-spoke wheels with centre-lock, knock-off hubs. Sweeping clamshell fenders were almost level with a hood that was twice the length of the engine. Free standing headlamps nestled between hood and fenders.

Tom McCahill, *Mechanix Illustrated* magazine's inimitable car tester, drove a TC in 1949 (MI 1/49). He called it a "gentleman of distinction," and judged its looks as "sporty, expensive and intriguing as a night on the Orient Express."

Alas the TC's obsolete chassis, rough ride and right-hand drive were out of tune with the times, especially in North America, the main export target. Thus after 10,000 TCs were built, the MG Car Co. ceased production in December 1949 and switched over to the TD model.

The MG TD Midget was more modern in appearance and design. Much to the displeasure of some purists, the TC's big wire wheels were replaced by 15-inch steel disc types. These were, as McCahill observed, "more functional and stronger – then so is a good tooth, but how many people prefer them?" Fenders were lower and the body lines were softer and less vertical.

Under the TD's "Americanized" styling could be found the independent coil spring front suspension from the MG Y-Series sedan. More precise rack and pinion steering replaced the cam and lever type, and an adjustable telescoping steering column was standard. Rear leaf springs were softened and given more travel for a better ride.

Although hard core enthusiasts scorned the less aesthetically "pure" TD, it was a better car in almost every way. It had a softer ride and wasn't as skittish in corners, and top speed was improved to 130 km/h (81 mph), according to *Road & Track* magazine (4/51).

The TD had the same 2388 mm (94 in.) wheelbase and 3683 mm (145 in.) overall length as the TC, but at 914 kg (2015 lb) it was almost 136 kg (300 lb) heavier. The TD's smaller wheels, which gave an effective lower gear ratio, just cancelled its extra weight, with the result that both the TC and TD's zero to 96 km/h (60 mph) times were in the 21 to 23 second range. To put this in perspective, Tom McCahill reported that his 1949 Ford V-8 could sprint to 96 (60) in 15.9 seconds.

When the TD arrived in North America it quickly consolidated the beachhead established by the TC. Its export model left-hand drive was very welcome, as were its better ride, roomier cockpit, and placement of both the speedometer and tachometer in front of the driver. In the TC the speedometer was in front of the passenger.

Like the TCs, TDs were raced and rallied. Sports car clubs were joined, and a general mood of esoteric camaraderie existed among MG owners. There was an unsaid feeling that sports car drivers were a little more "with it," that they had a keener appreciation for the finer mechanical things of life.

For those seeking more performance, the company soon offered the TD Mark II, a factory hop up with such modifications as higher compression, larger carburetors and valves, a higher axle ratio, and a second set of shock absorbers. Power was increased from 54 at 5200 rpm to 60 at 5500. According to *Road & Track* (2/53), the Mark II was approximately four km/h (two mph) faster, and about 3.0 seconds quicker to 96 km/h (60 mph).

While the MG TD was a favourite among sports car enthusiasts, it was becoming apparent as the fifties proceeded that the TD was falling seriously behind in performance. This was brought sharply into focus with the arrival of the Triumph TR2 which began landing here in 1953. For only a few hundred dollars more, the TR2 with its 2.0 litre, 90 horsepower engine, offered a top speed of 166 km/h (103 mph) and a zero to 96 (60) time of 12.2 seconds (*Road & Track* 4/54).

The TR2's envelope body, while not a paragon of fine styling, was still much more modern in appearance than the square-cut MG. After four years in which almost 30,000 were built, the

1955 MG TF 1500, end of the T-series line

market was forcing the MG Car Co. to discontinue the beloved TD.

MG's response was the 1954 TF, a transitional model that retained the angularity of the T-Series; it was really a TD that bowed to modernity with restyled front and rear ends. The hood was narrowed and the grille sloped back more sharply. Headlamps were moulded into the fenders. At the rear the spare tire and fuel tank were given more rake.

While the TF was a lovely little car, its archaic aerodynamics and only three extra horsepower meant that performance was still modest. Realizing that it was uncompetitive, MG quickly increased the cylinder bore from 66.5 to 72.0 mm (2.62 to 2.835 in.) by giving it "siamesed" cylinders which were no longer completely surrounded by coolant. This revised engine, called the XPEG, upped the TF's displacement to 1466 cc, and horsepower to 65. Thus equipped, the TF 1500 arrived for 1955.

While the TF 1500 could top 137 km/h (85 mph) and sprint to 96 (60) in 16.3 seconds (*Road & Track* 12/54), it was still no match for the Triumph.

The TF was the swan song of the T-Series MGs. Although popular – just under 10,000 were built in its two year run – it was clear that a more modern car was required if MG was to retain its reputation as the soul of the sports car movement. The TF was replaced by the full envelope bodied MGA for 1956.

While not particularly fast, T-Series MGs were loved and revered by sports car enthusiasts. They laid the groundwork for the sports car movement in North America, and paved the way for those that came after. T-type MGs are fondly remembered by those who owned them, and avidly collected by those who regard them as a high water mark in affordable fun.

MORGAN MOTOR COMPANY

In an automotive world dominated by computerization, automation and instant communications, it's refreshing to find an enterprise that still employs the traditional skills and ingenuity of dedicated wood workers, panel beaters and leather crafters.

That's the way it is at the Morgan Motor Company in Malvern Link, a town nestled among England's Malvern Hills in Worcestershire, some 190 kilometres (118 miles) north-west of London. And that's the way it has been for 90 years.

You won't find any assembly lines at Malvern Link; the cars are simply pushed on their own wheels from the "tin" shop to the paint shop to the trim shop. Nor will you find any engine labs staffed by white-coated engineers. You may even be hard pressed to find a computer.

What you will find is a staff of skilled artisans methodically turning metal, wood and leather into classically styled Morgan roadsters with long narrow hoods and clamshell fenders. They rollout of the low, red-brick factory on Picker-sleigh Road at the rate of 10 per week, and are eagerly snapped up by a clientele so imbued with Morgan magic they are willing to wait up to five years for a new "Moggie."

The Morgan tradition dates back to 1910, and the vision and ingenuity of a vicar's son who took up engineering rather than follow his father H.G. Morgan into the cloth. Henry Frederick Stanley Morgan (he became known as HFS in the motor industry), born in 1881, studied engineering at the Crystal Palace Engineering College in south London. He then took a job as a draughtsman with the Great Western Railway.

HFS had an early interest in automobiles, and in 1901 bought an Eagle three-wheeler. He turned that interest into a vocation when he and a partner opened a garage in Malvern Link in 1906. It was successful enough that they soon opened a second one in Worcester.

Morgan was sure that he could improve on the engineering of the Eagle and other existing designs, and with his business prospering, he was now able to pursue building his own car.

His first effort, a single seater completed in 1909, was a kind of cross between a motorcycle and a car. It was a three-wheeler fitted with a seven horsepower Peugeot motorcycle engine mounted between the front wheels.

The front suspension was an ingenious sliding-pillar-and-coil-spring type that HFS had adapted from a pioneering French Decauville design. It proved so well engineered and durable that its basic configuration has been used in every Morgan built until 1999. Not many engineering designs endure for 90 years!

Morgan showed two prototype single seater Morgans at the 1910 Motor Cycle Show at the Olympia exhibition hall in London. Although generating considerable interest, only about five orders were received. It so discouraged HFS's partner that he departed the business.

HFS looked for someone to build the cars for him, but was unsuccessful, so he formed the Morgan Motor Co. in 1910. His father provided financial backing, and became the company's first chairman.

The motorcycle show had taught HFS two important lessons: he must change his car to a two-seater; and he must gain publicity by demonstrating the speed and durability of his cars in competition.

HFS entered a single seater in the first London-to-Exeter two-day trial held on Boxing Day 1910. The JAP-engined Morgan won a gold medal, and received good publicity in the media. Additional competition successes led to many more orders when Morgan displayed his cars at the 1911 motorcycle show.

An important Morgan trait was a good power to weight ratio. This was at the heart of its racing accomplishments, and with more and more competition successes in the hands of both private owners and factory entries, the Morgan name built a solid reputation. Following a victory in the first Cyclecar Grand Prix of France, Morgan introduced its Grand Prix model in 1913. It was an immediate sales success, particularly in France, and would be made until 1926.

Morgan's three wheelers used a variety of air and water cooled side valve and overhead valve motorcycle and car engines, including JAP, Anzani, Blackburn, Matchless and Ford. A few light commercial vehicles were also produced.

In 1919 Morgan expanded its line and widened its appeal with the introduction of its four-seater Family model at the Olympia motor show. This configuration had been experimented with as early as 1912, but other priorities, such as military work for the First World War, had prevented its development.

The Family was followed in 1920 by the very popular Aero model with its tiny semi-circular aero windscreens. It was later expanded to a four-seater Aero Family model. The Aero was replaced by the Super Sports in the late 1920s.

In spite of the arrival of small four-wheel cars in the twenties, such as the Austin Seven and the

1932 Morgan Super Sport, for three-wheel aficionados

model "F" three-wheeler introduced at the 1933 motorcycle show had the potential to be expanded to a four-wheeler. It was powered by a Ford side-valve, four cylinder car engine.

It didn't take long for Morgan to change the F to four wheels. This was accomplished by spreading the frame members at the rear, and fitting a car rear axle and suspension. For more power, a 1.1 litre Coventry Climax inlet-over-exhaust four was used, and the 4-4 (four wheels, four cylinders) model was introduced in 1935. A four-seater version was developed for 1938 by relocating the battery and fuel tank, and making the luggage space smaller. Three-wheeled Morgans would continue to be offered until 1951, when demand finally disappeared.

Morris Minor, there continued to be a market for three-wheelers primarily because of the British tax system. Since three-wheelers were not considered "real" cars, they were taxed at the motorcycle rate, about half that of four-wheelers. When much of that tax advantage disappeared in 1935 it was a severe blow to Morgan. Although it did continue to produce three-wheelers, others such as BSA and Raleigh got out of the business.

With the trend clearly away from three-wheelers - Morgan's production fell from more than a 1000 in 1929 to 286 in 1935 - Morgan began to think of adding a fourth wheel. Its

Following the hiatus in car building during the Second World War, Morgan returned to production in 1947 with the 4/4 (now for some inexplicable reason, with a slash [/] instead of a dash [-]). With the former Coventry Climax engine no longer available, the 4/4 was powered by a 1.3 litre Standard four.

Then in 1951 Morgan introduced the Plus 4, a car that would be its mainstay until 1968. It was powered by Standard's new 2088 cc overhead valve Vanguard sedan engine that was also used in the Ferguson tractor. This engine continued until 1954.

When the Triumph TR2 sports car arrived in 1953 with the Vanguard engine slightly reduced in displacement to 1991 cc, and beefed up to 90 horsepower, Morgan started using it. Morgan would move on to the TR3, TR4 and TR4A versions until Standard discontinued it in 1968.

1952 Morgan Plus 4, keeping tradition alive

A significant change in appearance came in the mid-fifties when the free-standing headlamps Morgan had been using were no longer available. This necessitated moulding the headlamps into the fenders, and giving the grille a curved rather than a flat face.

To provide a lower priced sports car, Morgan revived the 4/4 model in 1955, again powered by a little Ford side-valve four. The 4/4 has continued to be offered, changing to later versions of Ford engines as they were developed.

Morgan even temporarily succumbed to the lure of modern aerodynamic styling in 1964 with the introduction of the fibreglass bodied coupe (a first for Morgan) called the Plus 4 Plus, a model that bore some Lotus cues. It wasn't really accepted as a Morgan, and only 26 were produced before the experiment was discontinued after just three years.

In 1966 the Rover Co. made an overture to Morgan regarding whether Morgan would sell out to them. This advance was rebuffed, but Peter Morgan, HFS's son who had become chairman upon his father's death in 1959, turned the tables

1959 Morgan Plus 4 four-seater, family sports car

and said they might be interested in Rover's V-8 engine. Rover had just acquired the 3.5 litre, aluminum pushrod V-8 from General Motors, which no longer required it for its Buick-Oldsmobile-Pontiac intermediates.

A deal was consummated for the V-8, and the Morgan Plus 8 was born. Little more than a Plus 4 stretched to accommodate a V-8 engine, it was introduced at London's 1968 Earls Court Motor Show.

The combination of Morgan's light construction, resulting in a curb weight of only 909 kg (2005 lb), and the urging of 184 horsepower, re-sulted in quick performance. *Road & Track* magazine recorded a zero to 96 km/h (60 mph) time of 8.5 seconds. The Plus 8's traditional Morgan brick-like aerodynamics kept the top speed at only 169 km/h (105 mph).

Morgan brought back the Plus 4 in 1985, now powered by a 2.0-litre Fiat engine. Production with this engine ended in 1987, and it was replaced in 1988 with a 16-valve Rover four.

In 1999 Morgan offered three models: the 2.0-litre Plus 4 in two-and four-seaters; the 1.8 litre 4/4 two-seater; and the 3.9-litre (or optional 4.6) powered Plus 8 two-seater. In a bow to modernity, a new aerodynamic model, the Aero 8, which makes extensive use of aluminum and is powered by a BMW engine, was introduced early in 2000.

Morgans have not been imported into Canada or the U.S. (except for a few compressed gas models) for several years because of government safety restrictions. This is an ironic twist because it was the North American market that saved Morgan when European demand dropped off in the sixties. The Morgan company is working to overcome this, and Morgans are expected to return to the North American market early in the 21st century.

In the meantime, the little factory on Picker-sleigh Road, where tradition is the watchword, continues to roll out its apparently timeless machines. They go to customers in many parts of the world who cherish the character of classic craftsmanship over the automated anonymity of mass production.

OLDSMOBILE AT 100

Oldsmobile celebrated it 100th anniversary in 1997 as the oldest continuously operating American automobile maker. It also had a long tradition of outstanding technical achievements.

Oldsmobile was created by Ransom Eli Olds, born on June 3, 1864 in Geneva, Ohio. The family moved to Lansing, Michigan in 1880 where they started P. F. Olds and Son (Wallace, not Ransom was the son) to repair machinery and build steam engines. Young Ransom joined the family firm in 1883, buying out Wallace in 1885 to become the "Son."

Business prospered, and the futuristic Ransom completed a crude, three-wheel, steam-powered vehicle in 1887. He followed this up in 1892 with a four-wheel

1903 Oldsmobile Curved Dash, popularized in song

steam car which the publicity conscious Ransom was able to have featured in the *Scientific American*.

While steam was established, Olds favoured gasoline engines, and also tried electricity. He received a patent for a "vapor engine" and built his first gasoline engine powered vehicle in 1896. The Olds Motor Works was founded on August 21, 1897, which is recognized as Oldsmobile's birthday. Four cars were produced that year.

The Olds Motor Works moved from Lansing to Detroit in 1900, and a disastrous 1901 plant fire destroyed all of the company's cars except a little Curved Dash gasoline model. Olds got back into business building this one cylinder car, with the Oldsmobile name being adopted in 1901. This 700 pound (318 kg) runabout with the toboggan-shaped front proved reliable, and was an immediate success. Olds was enticed back to Lansing by local businessmen in 1902 where large-scale Curved Dash production began.

The Curved Dash had vaulted into public prominence in 1901 when Oldsmobile test driver Roy Chapin drove one from Detroit to the New York auto show in 7-1/2 days, averaging 14 mph (22 km/h). It was the show's sensation, so impressing the Cleveland distributor that he ordered 1000 cars, an unheard of number in those days. The Curved Dash ultimately sold in 18 countries.

The Curved Dash was built until 1907, by which time it had been replaced by bigger, sturdier models. Output reached 4000 in 1903, making it the largest American motor vehicle producer for the third straight year. There were over 5500 built in 1905. The Curved Dash even inspired a popular song, "In My Merry Oldsmobile," by Gus Edwards and Vincent Bryan. A modified Curved Dash, the "Pirate," set a land speed record for its class of 54.38 mph on Ormond Beach, Florida in 1903.

Disagreeing with the board's decision to build bigger, heavier cars, Olds left the company in 1904, and went on to establish a car company called Reo, a name derived from his initials. This was the same year that two Curved Dashes, "Old Steady" and "Old Scout," made a coast-to-coast run covering 4000 miles (6440 km) in 44 days to focus attention on the need for better roads.

After Ransom's departure Oldsmobile's fortunes were mixed. Although introducing a two cylinder, then a four, and in 1908, a six, the company was in financial difficulty by 1908. Billy Durant bought it in November as part of the new General Motors Co. he had founded on September 16, 1908.

Oldsmobile soon moved into the luxury market with such cars as the Limited, powered by a huge 707 cubic inch (11.6 litre), 60 horsepower six. It had 42-inch wheels and a 138 inch (3505 mm) wheelbase, and this colossal car could reach about 70 mph (113 km/h).

It was soon decided that Oldsmobile's place was in the medium priced market, and there it began to progress. It introduced its first V-8 engine in 1916, which it made until 1923. By 1924 it had settled down to sixes, although it introduced another V-8 powered "companion" car, the Viking, in 1929, which was killed by the Depression in 1930.

Although losing money in 1930, '31 and '32, Oldsmobile made it through the Depression with a solid line of six and eight cylinder cars. It got independent front suspension in 1934, an all-steel "Turret Top" in 1935, and the "Safety Automatic Transmission" in 1938. This semi-automatic transmission anticipated one of the most

1934 Oldsmobile convertible coupe, middle class luxury

significant advancements in the history of the automobile: Oldsmobile's fully automatic four-speed "Hydra-Matic" transmission of 1940.

Following World War II's interruption in car production, during which Oldsmobile produced such items as ammunition, machine guns and tank canons, it returned to building pre-war designs while working on new models. It developed a sturdy, compact, short-stroke, overhead valve V-8 with a high compression ratio. Based on the work of GM's brilliant research chief Charles Kettering, it gave both more power and better fuel economy.

The introduction of this 135 horsepower "Rocket" engine in the new 1949 "88" model made Oldsmobile one of the world's best performing cars. It paced the Indianapolis 500 in 1949, won the first Mexican Road Race in 1950, and on the National Association for Stock Car Auto Racing circuits, won six of the nine NASCAR races in 1949, and 20 of 41 in 1951.

The 88 was also a winner in the showroom, helping move Oldsmobile into the lead in mid-price sales, and fourth in the industry (it would reach third in 1972).

Like many other American cars, Oldsmobiles grew big, powerful and glitzy in the 1950s. Its most significant car of the decade was the ultra luxurious 1953 Fiesta convertible. This image car, along with Cadillac's Eldorado and Buick's Skylark, introduced the wraparound "panoramic" windshield. The beloved creation of GM's legendary chief stylist Harley Earl, it swept the industry, and then disappeared within a decade.

In 1961 the F-85, Oldsmobile's version of GM's intermediate cars, was introduced with an aluminum 215 cubic inch (3.5 litre) V-8. The F-85 launched the Cutlass name, one of the most enduring, best selling of all Oldsmobiles. The F-85 also brought Oldsmobile's pioneering exhaust-driven turbo-supercharger in the 1962 Jetfire sports coupe, beating Chevrolet's turbocharged

Corvair Spyder to market by a month.

Although used in racing and commercial applications, Olds was the first to apply turbocharging to a production car. But it was cheaper to obtain more power by building a bigger engine, and the turbocharged 215 cubic inch, 215 horsepower V-8 was discontinued in 1963. Rover of England bought it for use in Rover cars

1940 Oldsmobile "Hydra-Matic" sedan, pioneers the fully automatic transmission

and sport utility vehicles such as the Range Rover.

Oldsmobile stunned the industry with its 1966 front-wheel drive Toronado. Although used widely in Europe, and by America's Cord in the 1930s, Oldsmobile revived front drive in North America, laying the groundwork for GM's mass changeover to FWD in the 1980s.

Rising safety concerns led Oldsmobile to introduce the first production airbag in the 1974 Toronado. Airbags soon disappeared, however, and it would be more than a decade before they would return. And driven by the 1973-74 energy crisis caused by the Arab oil embargo, Oldsmobile marketed the first American diesel car in 1978. Based on a converted 350 cubic inch (5.7 litre) gasoline V-8, it was a mixed blessing, being discontinued in 1985 after falling fuel economy concerns substantially reduced the diesel's appeal.

Fuel economy concerns in the late seventies and 1980s led GM to use more four and six cylinder engines. When GM re-entered the twin

1949 Oldsmobile "Rocket" 88, begins modern performance era

overhead camshaft, four-valves-per-cylinder engine business (the 1975-76 4-valve Chevrolet Cosworth Vega had been largely unsuccessful), Oldsmobile developed the Quad-4. This 2.3 litre 150 horsepower inline four bowed in the 1988 Oldsmobile Cutlass Calais, and soon spread to other divisions.

Following the General Motors trend, Oldsmobile gradually phased out its rear-wheel drive cars; the last rear drive Cutlass was built in 1990. It

1963 Oldsmobile F-85 Jetfire turbocharged coupe

173

1966 Oldsmobile Toronado, front-wheel drive from The General

entered the sport-utility business in 1991 with the Bravada.

In harking back to its good old V-8 days, now with front-wheel drive, Oldsmobile introduced its luxury class 1995 Aurora powered by a 4.0 litre version of Cadillac's Northstar double over-head cam, 32-valve V-8. It developed 250 horse-power, enough to propel the 4,000 pound (1814 kg) sedan in a sprightly fashion.

Rumours circulated in the 1990s that the Oldsmobile Division would be phased out. But just as Mark Twain called the report of his demise greatly exaggerated, we hope the rumours of Oldsmobile's demise are equally false. It would be sad to see America's oldest automaker, one with such a legacy of engineering innovation, disap-pear from the scene.

THE RUSSELL

Canada has produced few genuine home-grown motor vehicles. It built foreign designs almost exclusively, predominantly from the United States. The Russell was one of the truly native Canadian cars, designed and manufactured in Toronto. There was a Cleveland-produced American Russell car made from 1902 to 1904, but it was not related to the Canadian Russell.

The history of the Russell dates back to the turn of the century. In 1902 Canadian Motors

1907 Russell, Canada's indigenous car

Ltd. (CML), located at 710 Yonge St. in Toronto, was in financial difficulties. It had been operating for a couple of years with some success, making and selling cars, and even exporting some to England, but sales hadn't been strong enough to make it a viable enterprise. New money was needed or the company would be finished.

CML's financial angel came in the form of the Canada Cycle and Motor Co. CCM had been formed in 1899 through the amalgamation of several bicycle companies, including the bicycle wing of the great Massey-Harris farm implement company, and the H.A. Lozier Co., a Toledo bicycle manufacturer (it would later go into cars) which also had a Canadian plant in West Toronto. But CCM suffered when the bicycle craze came to an end. CCM's famous tubular ice skates, called "Automobile Skates," were still a few years in the future.

As a result of the bicycle downturn, Thomas Alexander Russell, CCM's new, young general manager, was forced to take the company through a drastic consolidation.

Tommy Russell, an honours political science graduate from the University of Toronto, was quiet, capable and shrewd. He had joined the company as secretary in 1901, but his talents soon resulted in his appointment as general manager. He proved to be a good manager, and quickly recognized that to prosper the company needed a new product. He was also prescient enough to recognize that the motor car was emerging as a viable transportation machine.

Manufacturing cars wasn't totally new to CCM. The company had recently built a few spindly motorized "tricycles," called Mottettes, and "quadracycles." They were powered by French De Dion gasoline engines that had become available through the acquisition of Lozier. Also, for a couple of years CCM had controlled the National Cycle and Automobile Co., which built American-designed Locomobile steam cars in Hamilton.

By 1903 Russell had the Yonge Street plant turning out an electrically powered two-passenger runabout called the Ivanhoe. Production lasted until 1905, but even before that, Russell could see that the electric car had its limitations. He believed that the gasoline engine would be the automobile power of choice.

A new Russell car, the model A, powered by a flat, two cylinder gasoline engine, was brought out in 1905. It had such advanced features as a front-mounted engine, shaft drive and a sliding-gear transmission with a column-mounted shift lever.

In their book, *Cars of Canada*, Hugh Durnford and Glenn Baechler estimate that only about 25 model A Russells were built. But, in spite of this it did confirm that Russell was dedicated to building a quality product, and established a good reputation for the marque.

This was followed in 1906 by a larger model B, and a four-cylinder model C Russell, which further consolidated Russell's quest for quality. The added models necessitated a bigger factory, and the enterprise was relocated to more spacious premises on Weston Road at McCormack Street in the Toronto Junction.

Tommy Russell exploited nationalism by emphasizing the Canadian aspect of the cars, advertising them as "The Thoroughly Canadian Car," with Canadian material, Canadian labour, and Canadian capital.

The model B and C Russells proved to be such well-built and soundly engineered cars that the Dominion Automobile Co., which marketed Russells, soon opened sales offices in England, Australia and New Zealand. Now the advertisements became even more lavish: "Three continents attest to Russell's excellence," they boasted.

The value of publicity was not lost on CCM, and it engaged in such stunts as racing a Russell against an ice-yacht on frozen Lake Ontario (the Russell won), and driving one for two hours in bitterly cold weather with only water in the radiator (they didn't dare let it stop).

There was increasing success and Russell models proliferated. A big 40-horsepower touring car was added in 1907, then an even more prestigious 50-horsepower model in 1908. They also expanded into the commercial vehicle field with delivery trucks, buses, ambulances and fire trucks.

Russell cars were quickly moving up the social scale, in the process leaving the popular price range to others. This was a common occurrence at that time because there were two schools of thought on automobiles: that cars should be economical, and affordable to the masses, or that they should be heavy and expensive because only the wealthy could afford them anyway. Henry Ford and Ransom Olds were on the side of the light affordable car, which ultimately would prove the more prosperous path.

The Russell company chose to go upmarket. Thus, when Tommy Russell heard about the new sleeve-valve engine that had been invented by Charles Yale Knight of Chicago in 1903, he thought it would be ideal for the luxury image he was cultivating for his cars. In spite of its much lower noise level, Knight had been unable to sell American manufacturers on his engine, so he decided to try interesting European car builders in it.

The big advantage of the Knight engine was its quietness. Conventional poppet valves and valve gear at that time were still primitive and noisy. The sleeve-valve engine, in which the sleeves encircled the pistons and slid quietly up and down, were almost noiseless. Russell wanted the silent running of the sleeve-valve engine because it would add a real touch of luxury to his cars.

In 1906 Knight set sail for Europe in an attempt to convince luxury carmakers to use his idea. Among others, England's Daimler, France's

1911 Russell, Knight model 38

successful, and the first Knight-equipped Russell model, the "Silent-Knight," was introduced in 1910. It was the first North American car to use the Knight engine.

New models and plant expansions carried the company from strength to strength until it was the Russell tail wagging the CCM dog. Thus, in 1911 it became the Russell Motor Car Co., with CCM as a branch.

Then in 1913 company fortunes began to turn down. The sleeve-valve engine that had fared so well on the test bench gave some trouble in the field in the form of such things as broken sleeves and excessive oil consumption. In spite of a valiant attempt by Tommy Russell, with new models and strenuous testing of the sleeve valve engine in the engineering laboratory of the University of Toronto, the company ceased building cars in 1916.

Although Russell tried to move back into the low-priced market, it was too late. An economic downturn, and World War I, combined to end their car-building.

Panhard, Belgium's Minerva, and Germany's Daimler-Motoren-Gesellschaft, maker of the Mercedes, all builders of prestige cars, adopted the Knight engine.

Daimler ran some exhaustive tests on the Knight engine. Tommy Russell had been following the fortunes of Charles Knight and his new powerplant. When he heard the remarkable results of these tests, he was so impressed that he was soon on a ship to England to find Knight and obtain Canadian rights to the engine. Russell was

The car-making part of the Russell company was sold to John North Willys of Toledo, Ohio, whose Willys-Knight would popularize the sleeve-valve engine. Willys-Overland would make more sleeve-valve cars than all other manufacturers combined, and would build cars in the old Russell plant into the 1930s. The Russell company continued with military work until the end of the war, and eventually became a holding company for several prominent Canadian firms.

Tommy Russell went on to even greater prominence as the president of the Massey-Harris farm implement company, a position he held for many years. He died in 1940, leaving behind, among other good things, the legacy of having built the most truly Canadian car.

TORONTO AS A MOTOR CITY

When one thinks of the great motoring industry cities of the world – places like Detroit, Coventry, and Turin – Toronto doesn't come to mind. But although the Ontario capital ranks well down as a motor city, Toronto has over the years produced a surprising number of cars. Just as Indianapolis, Indiana, almost became the Detroit of America, Toronto could well have been the Oshawa, Windsor or Oakville of Canada. She was after all, the birthplace of more than a dozen different makes of cars.

Some of these, of course, were American designs, only assembled in Toronto, but some of the nameplates were as genuinely homegrown Canadian as the beaver and the maple leaf. And some manufacturers were successful for awhile; others, alas, could claim an entire production of only one vehicle.

When we look at Toronto's automobile building history it is appropriate to start in the beginning with the very first car. In 1893 the Dixon Carriage Works, located at the corner of Bay and Temperance Streets, produced what could have been called either the Dixon or the Featherstonhaugh.

This electric carriage was built for a prominent Toronto lawyer named Fred Featherstonhaugh,

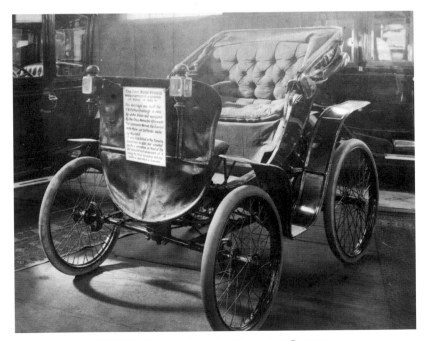

1893 Featherstonhaugh – Toronto's first car

and was featured at the 1893 Canadian National Exhibition. Electric power seemed to be the way of the future because it was just a year earlier that the Toronto Railway Company had electrified its first section of track on Church Street.

The Dixon/Featherstonhaugh came about when Mr. Featherstonhaugh, a patent attorney and somewhat of a futurist, was approached by a British-born engineer by the name of William Still. Still had developed a light and efficient electric storage battery which he wanted to patent, and sought out the attorney for that purpose.

They soon discovered their mutual interest in the automobile, which had been invented in Europe a few years earlier, and was starting to emerge in North America. Although steam power was then at its peak, Featherstonhaugh wasn't interested in it because of the heat, heavy boiler, fuel and water requirements, and the complicated firing up process. It just wasn't his idea of a convenient runabout. This suited Still because electricity was his passion, and it wasn't long before Featherstonhaugh asked Still if he could design a power system to go with his efficient new battery.

It was just the kind of challenge that the inventive Mr. Still enjoyed, and he soon had an electric power system developed to meet Featherstonhaugh's exacting standards.

The Dixon Carriage Works was commissioned to build a car using Still's powertrain. It was a good choice because John Dixon turned out a fine product. Riding on pneumatic tires and stylish wire-spoke wheels, the Dixon/Featherstonhaugh boasted a folding top and electric lights long before they were popular. The throttle was integrated into the steering tiller, and considering that this was one of Canada's earliest cars, and the first electric, it was a marvel of technology. It would also prove to be durable, as Mr. Featherstonhaugh continued to drive it for some 15 years.

The success of the Featherstonhaugh car prompted a group of Toronto businessmen to organize the Canadian Motor Syndicate with William Still as its engineer. The real strength of the enterprise was Still's patents, and the syndicate was able to show three vehicles, including Featherstonhaugh's, at the 1898 Canadian National Exhibition. One of the others was a kind of motorized wicker love seat with two wheels in front and one at the rear. The third vehicle was a delivery tricycle with a large cargo box behind the driver. In addition to these electrics, Still built a gasoline fueled vehicle powered by a five horsepower air cooled engine, but his heart was never really in it; electricity was his love.

The loosely organized syndicate didn't last long, and a new firm, the Still Motor Company, was set up in May 1899 at 710-724 Yonge Street. Electricity was still the motive power, and they produced a variety of vehicles, including delivery wagons and the wicker tricycle. But fortune did not smile on the Still company, and by 1900 it was out of capital.

New financing came from un unusual source, Great Britain, perhaps because of Still's background, and the company rose again as Canadian Motors Limited. With British financing came British sales, and CML exported several models. One of these, inelegantly called the Dog Cart at home, was exported to England as the Oxford, a much more refined name.

One other Toronto company attempted to produce a car commercially prior to the turn of the century. The McLachlan Electric and Gasoline Motor Company Limited, located at 94 Adelaide Street West, produced one gasoline vehicle in 1899 based on the German Benz. It proved unsuccessful and no more were built. The MaLachlan name, by the way, should not be confused with the famous Sam McLaughlin of Oshawa, Ontario whose carriage company went into automobile building, and went on to become General Motors of Canada.

Shortly after this, in 1901, a new Toronto-built car appeared on the scene. It was the Queen, manufactured by the Queen City Cycle and Motor Works at 304 Queen Street West. The Queen was modern enough to have a steering wheel, and the driver sat behind the two front passengers.

The Queen apparently had a few shortcomings for potential customers, the worst of which was a tendency to toss its passengers onto the road when the transmission gears were shifted. The engine was also prone to catching fire. These problems proved difficult for the manufacturer to explain away, and it's unlikely that more than one Queen was produced. Perhaps one was enough.

While British capital and sales kept Canadian Motors Limited functioning for a couple of years, it folded again in 1902. The Yonge Street property seemed to be doomed for car production until another saviour, Canada Cycle and Motor, stepped in to rescue it.

Things were not going well for CCM due to the collapsing bicycle market brought on by the end of the cycling fad of the 1890s. And the tubular ice skate that would make CCM a household name in sporting circles was still a few years away. The company was undergoing a drastic consolidation under its capable new general manager, Thomas Alexander Russell.

The company was not entirely new to car building, having recently completed several spindly looking "tricycles," (called Motettes) and "quadracycles" powered by small gasoline engines.

CCM had evolved out of an amalgamation of, among others, the bicycle wing of the great Massey-Harris farm implement company, and H.A. Lozier & Company, a bicycle and car manufacturer. With Lozier, M-H also got the rights to the Locomobile steam car that was being built in Hamilton. CCM was controlled by Massey-

Harris, and the new little vehicles carried that name. They had French de Dion engines for which M-H had obtained the rights through its acquisition of Lozier. The Canadian Post Office bought several of these Massey- Harrises for use in the mail service.

Tommy Russell was a heads-up executive who saw a great future for the automobile business. In 1903 the 710 Yonge Street plant began turning out a new CCM car, the Ivanhoe. It was an electric, but one with a Canadian innovation: some of the batteries were located in the rear of the vehicle, and some in the front for better weight distribution. Production of this two passenger runabout lasted until 1905.

By this time it was becoming apparent to Russell and others that the internal combustion engine was rapidly gaining ground in reliability, so a gasoline engined car was designed. The first Russell, as the new car was called, appeared in 1905, and was a well engineered, small four passenger vehicle.

When Russell's car production ended in 1916 its factory in the Toronto Junction at Weston Road and McCormack Street was taken over by the Willys-Overland Company of Toledo, Ohio. W-O turned out Overland cars in the Weston Road facility from 1915 to 1918, when the plant was converted to the production of aircraft engines.

Automobile production resumed in 1919 with the new, small Overland four with an all-steel body. Deluxe trim was featured in 1922 for the Overland Special, and a more luxurious model was added in 1923 called the Bluebird. It was followed by the Redbird in 1924.

By 1926 a new car called the Whippet replaced the Overland, and in 1927 the company began producing the Willys-Knight with the sleeve-valve type engine that Russell cars had used. Whippets, particularly the four cylinder model, were popular in Canada, and the company flourished.

In spite of a new Whippet Superior being introduced in 1929 the onset of the Depression dealt Willys-Overland a heavy blow, as it did others. The Whippet name was replaced by Willys in 1930, but even with a new eight cylinder car, of which very few were built, and the adoption of more aerodynamic styling, the company succumbed to financial problems in 1933.

About the time the Russell company was experiencing difficulty in the early teens, another Canadian was conceiving a new idea to deal with the horrible roads of the day. Rather than trying to keep air in the questionable quality tires of that era, R.C. Bartlett reasoned that it would be much more practical to put the air in springs and mount them on the frame where they wouldn't be damaged. He decided that solid tires and air springs would be a better combination than the pneumatic tires and harsh steel suspensions then in use.

He even tried an independent front suspension system using an axle that was hinged in the middle, a system that would be successfully used by the English Allard many years later, but abandoned the idea. A millwright in the Northern Ontario mining industry, Bartlett patented the air suspension invention. With his fine reputation as a clever inventor, this natural engineer was able to organize a syndicate in Porcupine (now Timmins) to provide the finances for a pilot model.

In 1913 Bartlett came to Toronto and built the first prototype in a machine shop behind the King Edward Hotel. In addition to the air springs, the Bartlett had four-wheel brakes aided by spikes that protruded through the solid tires when the brakes were applied. This was before manufacturers had proving grounds, so testing was done on public roads. When the new brakes were tested on King Street the result was a multi-car crash, and a lot of damaged front ends on cars without the Bartlett's superior braking power.

In spite of this inauspicious start, Bartlett was able to organize the Canadian Bartlett Automobile Company Limited located in a rented garage at 1257 Queen Street West in Toronto. The company built its own bodies and used running gear imported from the U.S. Toronto production totalled approximately 100 cars before the operation moved to Stratford, Ontario, in 1916. Most

1932 Frontenac Sedan

Bartletts used the pneumatic air bladder suspension, an idea that was many decades ahead of its time. When its American parts supply dried up during the First World War, Bartlett was forced out of business in 1917.

It was also around this time, in 1914, that the Dart Cycle Car Company Limited was established in Toronto to assemble a Canadian version of the American Scripps-Booth cycle car. These light and flimsy cycle cars proved to be a short-lived craze, and the company built no more than a handful of vehicles.

Another name that came briefly on the Toronto automotive scene was the Jules Motor Company, named after its engineer Julius Hal-

1923 Star

tenberger. The company was established in Toronto in 1910, but it is uncertain whether any cars were actually built before the operation moved to Guelph, Ontario, in 1911. Two cars were eventually produced there. An unusual feature was that the horn button was in the middle of the brake pedal.

Another enterprise, the Ross Car Company, apparently existed in Toronto from 1911 to 1914. Production was reported to be two vehicles, a coupe and a runabout.

Toronto was also the home of Peck Electric Limited, which was formed in 1911, and located at the corner of Jarvis and Adelaide Streets. It made a rather elegant $4,000 electric, but in spite of the company's slogan that the car "Keeps Pecking," production continued only through 1913. It was doomed in part by the arrival of the electric starter for gasoline cars which Cadillac pioneered in 1912, and which sent electric and steam cars into rapid decline.

The Redpath, another limited production car, was built by a Toronto pattern maker by the name of Walter Redpath. The plant was started in Berlin (now called Kitchener), Ontario, in 1902, but moved to Toronto in about 1905. The company produced the one cylinder gasoline engined Redpath Messenger in very limited numbers until the factory burned in 1907.

After the First World War, events in the United States were to have an impact on the Toronto automobile scene. William Durant was the American super salesman and engaging entrepreneur who organized General Motors in 1908, lost control to the bankers in 1910, and regained it through Chevrolet in 1915. When he lost control for the second and last time in 1920, Durant almost immediately formed another company, Durant Motors Incorporated.

Recognizing a good market in Toronto and Canada, and familiar with his friend Sam McLaughlin's success in Oshawa, he came across the border and formed Durant Motors of Canada in 1921. He acquired a former munitions plant on Laird Drive at Wicksteed in the Leaside area of Toronto, and the first Durant car rolled out in the spring of 1922.

In the beginning the plant was largely an assembly operation, although this later changed as more and more components were manufactured in Canada. Soon another make, the Star, a low priced car to compete with the Ford Model T, was added. Thousands of Stars were built for export, where they were sold under the Rugby name.

Durant and Rugby trucks were also produced. The Star name was discontinued in 1928, replaced by the Frontenac in Canada.

By the late 1920s Durant's U.S. operation was losing money and sliding into debt. This led to the loss of its Canadian operation, which was reorganized with local funding to evolve into the fully Canadian owned Durant Motors of Canada. This became Dominion Motors Limited in 1931 turning out Durant cars and Rugby trucks.

Dominion Motors introduced a new four cylinder Frontenac in 1931. Although it was popular, the Depression was taking its toll and sales did not fare as well as had been hoped.

Dominion also assembled Reo Flying Clouds under licence for two years, but this wasn't enough to save the company, and production stopped in 1933. The last Toronto, and Canadian, automobile company was gone.

Not all of the Toronto auto nameplates were to fade into obscurity. Some present day North American companies were also part of the early Toronto car-building scene. The Ford Motor Company of Canada began assembling Model Ts on Dupont Street at Christie in about 1914, and continued operations there until 1923. Ford then erected a new plant at Danforth Avenue and Victoria Park Avenue on a 15-acre site purchased from the Grand Trunk Railway. It continued to build cars there until civilian production was shut down during the Second World War.

Dodge Brothers Canada Limited was another Toronto car builder. In 1925 Dodge set up manufacturing in a plant located at 1244 Dufferin Street. Production carried on there until Chrysler Canada moved it to Windsor in 1929, following the purchase of Dodge by the Chrysler Corporation in 1928.

There was to be more automobile production in Toronto soon after the Second World War. The Nash Motor Company of Kenosha, Wisconsin, bought the Ford plant on Danforth Avenue in 1946 and established Nash Motors of Canada Limited. It turned out Nashes, including the "inverted bathtub" Canadian Statesman, from 1950 to 1957, when the amalgamation of Nash and Hudson to form American Motors Corporation, and economic conditions, dictated that Toronto production cease.

The old Leaside plant was to have one more brief automotive fling when the Kaiser-Frazer

1951 Nash Canadian Statesman

Corporation of Willow Run, Michigan, set up Kaiser-Frazer of Canada Limited in 1950 to build cars. According to Perry Zavitz's book, *Canadian Cars, 1946-1984*, only 1359 1951 Kaisers, and one 1952 Kaiser, were produced before the Leaside operation was shut down.

This, then, is a summary of Toronto's automobile building history. There may have been other companies formed for the purpose of building cars, and a few may even have gone beyond blueprints to the prototype stage. They seem, however, to have been lost in the mists of time.

INDEX